B2+

SHORT COURSE SERIES

English for Tax Professionals

Patrick Mustu

Dieses Buch als E-Book nutzen:
Use this book as an e-book:
mein.cornelsen.de

33fy-ax-xu4j

English for
Tax Professionals

B2+

SHORT COURSE SERIES

Autor: Patrick Mustu
Beratende Mitwirkung:
Sarah A. Brown, Simon Schneider
Redaktion: Robert Baltzer

Umschlaggestaltung: Studio SYBERG, Berlin
Umschlagfoto: Shutterstock.com/Natee Meepian
Layoutkonzept: Studio SYBERG, Berlin
Layout und technische Umsetzung:
PER MEDIEN & MARKETING GmbH, Braunschweig

Bildquellen:
S. 3/1: Shutterstock.com/Andrey_Popov; **S. 3/2:** Shutterstock.com/Andrey_Popov; **S. 3/3:** Shutterstock.com/Golubovy; **S. 3/4:** Shutterstock.com/Funtap; **S. 3/5:** Shutterstock.com/TippaPatt; **S. 3/6:** Shutterstock.com/Photon photo; **S. 5/m.l.:** Shutterstock.com/Funtap; **S. 5/m.l.:** Shutterstock.com/Golubovy; **S. 5/o.l.:** Shutterstock.com/Andrey_Popov; **S. 5/u.l.:** Shutterstock.com/Photon photo; **S. 5/u.l.:** Shutterstock.com/TippaPatt; **S. 6:** Shutterstock.com/Andrey_Popov; **S. 8:** Shutterstock.com/fizkes; **S. 9:** Shutterstock.com/Stock 4you; **S. 10:** Shutterstock.com/dizain; **S. 13:** Shutterstock.com/sasirin pamai; **S. 14/m.r.:** Shutterstock.com/megaflopp; **S. 14/o.:** Shutterstock.com/Andrey_Popov; **S. 19:** Shutterstock.com/22Images Studio; **S. 21:** Shutterstock.com/Studio Romantic; **S. 22/m.l.:** Shutterstock.com/BearFotos; **S. 22/m.r.:** Shutterstock.com/Ground Picture; **S. 22/o.:** Shutterstock.com/Golubovy; **S. 23:** Shutterstock.com/Andrey_Popov; **S. 29:** Shutterstock.com/Erhan Inga; **S. 30:** Shutterstock.com/Funtap; **S. 36:** amtliches Werk; **S. 36:** Shutterstock.com/MandriaPix; **S. 37:** Shutterstock.com/Rawpixel.com; **S. 38/m.r.:** Shutterstock.com/Aun Photographer; **S. 38/o.:** Shutterstock.com/TippaPatt; **S. 41:** Shutterstock.com/fizkes; **S. 42:** Shutterstock.com/Olivier Le Moal; **S. 43:** amtliches Werk; **S. 45:** Shutterstock.com/New Africa; **S. 46:** Shutterstock.com/Photon photo; **S. 47:** Shutterstock.com/chase4concept; **S. 49:** Shutterstock.com/SFIO CRACHO; **S. 50:** Shutterstock.com/Jacob Lund; **S. 51:** Shutterstock.com/Circlephoto; **S. 53:** Shutterstock.com/Geobor.

www.cornelsen.de

1. Auflage, 1. Druck 2024

Basierend auf *English for Tax Professionals* (ISBN 978-3-464-20193-0)

Alle Drucke dieser Auflage sind inhaltlich unverändert und können im Unterricht nebeneinander verwendet werden.

© 2024 Cornelsen Verlag GmbH, Mecklenburgische Str. 53, 14197 Berlin

Das Werk und seine Teile sind urheberrechtlich geschützt. Jede Nutzung in anderen als den gesetzlich zugelassenen Fällen bedarf der vorherigen schriftlichen Einwilligung des Verlages. Hinweis zu §§ 60 a, 60 b UrhG: Weder das Werk noch seine Teile dürfen ohne eine solche Einwilligung an Schulen oder in Unterrichts- und Lehrmedien (§ 60 b Abs. 3 UrhG) vervielfältigt, insbesondere kopiert oder eingescannt, verbreitet oder in ein Netzwerk eingestellt oder sonst öffentlich zugänglich gemacht oder wiedergegeben werden. Dies gilt auch für Intranets von Schulen und anderen Bildungseinrichtungen.

Druck: Mohn Media Mohndruck, Gütersloh

ISBN: 978-3-06-123276-4 (Kursbuch)
Produktnummer: 1100034915 (E-Book)

PEFC-zertifiziert
Dieses Produkt stammt aus nachhaltig bewirtschafteten Wäldern und kontrollierten Quellen
PEFC/04-31-1033 www.pefc.de

TABLE OF CONTENTS

		TOPICS	LANGUAGE FUNCTIONS
	**1** **Introduction to taxation & auditing** Page 6	• Jobs in taxation & auditing • Areas of accounting • Professionals in the UK & US	• Meeting clients • Practising short conversations • Making small talk
	**2** **Advising employees** Page 14	• Deductions, allowances & benefits • Remote work • UK & US taxes	• Making appointments • Conducting interviews & giving advice • Drafting emails & memoranda
	**3** **Advising freelancers** Page 22	• Freelancers, traders & professionals • Starting & running your business • Expenses & tax accounting	• Explaining tax forms • Briefing clients • Visualising information
	**4** **Corporate taxation** Page 30	• Corporate structures • Trade tax • Financial statements	• Advising start-ups • Explaining corporate taxes • Analysing financial statements
	**5** **International taxation** Page 38	• VAT in EU trade • Taxing multinationals • Tax avoidance	• Tele- & videoconferencing • Explaining double taxation agreements • Discussing profit shifting
	**6** **Working in auditing** Page 46	• Types of auditing • Creative accounting • Reporting	• Explaining internal and external auditing • Giving presentations • Explaining non-financial reporting

Materials	Page 54	**Useful Phrases**	Page 69	**A-Z Wordlist**	Page 76
Transcripts	Page 57	**Correspondence**	Page 72	**Troubleshooting**	Page 78
Answer Key	Page 63	**Glossary**	Page 74	**Acronyms and Key Verbs**	Page 80

INTRODUCING
ENGLISH FOR TAX PROFESSIONALS

As you will know from your job, English plays an increasingly important role in international business communication. *English for Tax Professionals* will provide you with the communicative language needed for effective communication with clients, colleagues and business partners. It comes along with an array of technical terms covering various topics and settings.

English for Tax Professionals contains the following components designed to help you learn effectively.

- The book's six units cover a comprehensive range of important topics. As you can see from the table of contents on page 3, the aim here is to give a broad overview of what you need to know in a compact format.

- The wide range of exercises will provide you with ample practice and opportunities to learn key phrases and technical terms no matter your personal learning style.

- The book encourages regular discussion with other people in your English course. The discussion tasks are focused on giving you the opportunity to draw on your personal experience while practising key language.

- The simulations and mediation activities in each unit allow you to actively practise phrases and vocabulary in relevant scenarios. They encourage you to use and adapt the language learned to perform tasks as you would in the real world.

- 🔊 The listening tasks in every unit present a broad range of accents to prepare you for the way English is spoken internationally. The recordings can be accessed using the **Cornelsen Lernen App** or the **webcode "dixomi"** on **codes.cornelsen.de**.

- 📱 The **Cornelsen Lernen App** offers interactive exercises, which practise and expand on the useful phrases provided in this book. They are designed as a resource for independent learning.

- The appendix includes further materials, transcripts of the audio recordings, an answer key, a phrase bank with all useful phrases from this book, an overview on correspondence, a glossary explaining technical terms often encountered, an A-Z wordlist as a summary of the vocabulary boxes, an explanation on common mistakes as well as a list of acronyms and key verbs frequently used in the world of taxes. It is designed to help you to use the book in your own time as a resource for independent learning and for reference purposes.

- The **webcode** also offers teaching tips for further support.

The needs analysis on the next page will support you in setting personal learning goals at the outset of the book and assessing your progress once you have worked through it.

Best of luck with your English course.

Patrick Mustu
and the Cornelsen editorial team

NEEDS ANALYSIS

English for Tax Professionals is designed to improve your English-language skills for a wide range of tasks relevant to taxation, accounting and auditing. However, you are in the best position to know which skills you need to develop most to help you in your work.

Have a look at the list below and spend a few minutes ticking the skills that you consider most important. Which do you want to prioritize and improve? Add other skills to the list that you would like to concentrate on.

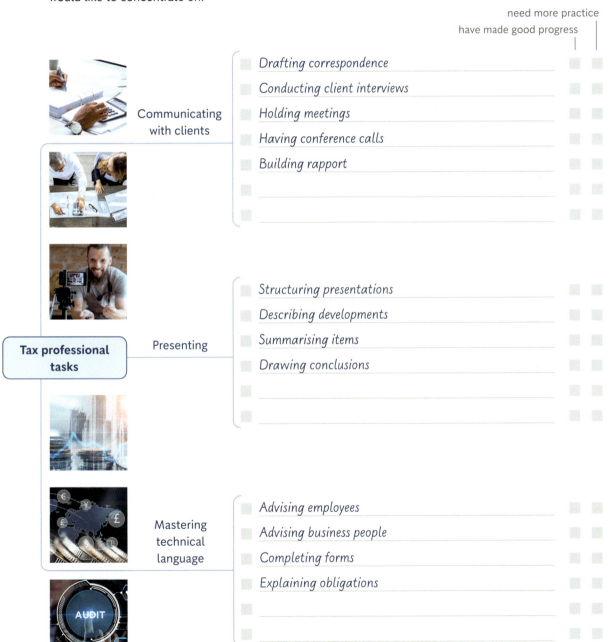

need more practice
have made good progress

Communicating with clients
- ☐ Drafting correspondence ☐ ☐
- ☐ Conducting client interviews ☐ ☐
- ☐ Holding meetings ☐ ☐
- ☐ Having conference calls ☐ ☐
- ☐ Building rapport ☐ ☐
- ☐ _____ ☐ ☐
- ☐ _____ ☐ ☐

Presenting
- ☐ Structuring presentations ☐ ☐
- ☐ Describing developments ☐ ☐
- ☐ Summarising items ☐ ☐
- ☐ Drawing conclusions ☐ ☐
- ☐ _____ ☐ ☐
- ☐ _____ ☐ ☐

Mastering technical language
- ☐ Advising employees ☐ ☐
- ☐ Advising business people ☐ ☐
- ☐ Completing forms ☐ ☐
- ☐ Explaining obligations ☐ ☐
- ☐ _____ ☐ ☐
- ☐ _____ ☐ ☐

Try to keep the skills you want to improve in mind while working with the book. Once you have completed it, turn back to this page and assess your progress.

IN THIS UNIT YOU WILL …
- discuss what accountants do
- look at accounting professionals in Germany, the UK and the US
- interact with a client

1 Introduction to taxation & auditing

 What does a tax advisor do? Complete the diagram, then compare and discuss yours with other members of the class.

advise individuals on personal taxation

TAX ADVISOR

1 Discuss the following questions.

1. What are typical issues tax advisors are faced with?
2. Who doesn't need tax advice and why? Are there clients who need tax advice more than others?
3. Can only tax advisors advise on tax issues or can other professionals/institutions do so too?

2 Fill in the gaps with the words from the box.

compete | corporate | estate | fee schedule | refund | represent | returns | limited company | opinions | partnership | payroll | public accountants | start-ups | trustees | VAT

Tax consultants give advice in tax and business administration matters and _____ [1] clients before tax offices and in finance courts. Tax advisors can also do bookkeeping and _____ [2] accounting. They prepare tax _____ [3] and inform whether to expect a _____ [4]. For companies, they draft financial statements and handle complex _____ [5] income tax and _____ [6] issues. They can advise

ENGLISH FOR TAX PROFESSIONALS

on _____⁷, asset management and social security matters. Tax advisors also act as _____⁸, draft _____⁹ and handle bankruptcies. They can help with _____¹⁰ planning. Payment of tax advisors is regulated by a statutory _____¹¹. Tax advisors either work on their own or form a _____¹², in some cases even a _____¹³. Tax advisors _____¹⁴ with other professionals. These include _____¹⁵, lawyers and certain associations.

> **VOCABULARY**
>
> **fee schedule** Gebührentabelle
> **opinion** *hier:* Gutachten
> **statutory** gesetzlich
> **trustee** Treuhänder

3 Tick the activities a German tax advisor cannot be involved in.

- ☐ Advising on social security matters
- ☐ Advising on start-ups
- ☐ Advising on the management of assets
- ☐ Auditing
- ☐ Checking tax assessments made by the tax or revenue office
- ☐ Doing bookkeeping
- ☐ Doing payroll accounting
- ☐ Giving general legal advice, e.g. on consumer law issues
- ☐ Giving advice on tax and business administration issues
- ☐ Preparing tax returns
- ☐ Representing clients before fiscal courts

> **DID YOU KNOW?**
>
> The usual English equivalent of *Steuerberater*in* is **tax advisor** (also spelled "tax adviser") or **tax consultant**, but many English speakers use the term **accountant**. This term is also used for professional auditors, or public accountants, in both the UK (**Chartered Accountants**) and the US (**Certified Public Accountants (CPAs)**). There are no formal requirements for giving tax advice or preparing returns in the UK or US. However, in the US, only certain professionals such as CPAs or attorneys (*Rechtsanwälte*) are allowed to act before the tax authorities.

4 Prepare a short talk on how to become a tax advisor in Germany that covers the questions below. Then present it to your group and discuss.

- What are the requirements in general?
- What are the options leading to the qualifying exam? What are the pros and cons?
- Which option did you choose?
- What does the exam look like in terms of scope and length? Why do so many people fail?

5 SIMULATION

Hold a meeting with your classmates, representing yourself in a meeting of tax professionals. Discuss tax issues you regularly/sometimes/never cover, what you specialise in, and what types of clients you advise. Take notes. Begin by introducing your firm (location, size, focus).

Regular issues	Rare issues	No issue

6 Make word combinations with 'tax' that match the following definitions.

allowance | assessment | bracket | ~~burden~~ | cut | deduction | hike | incentive | return | refund

1 tax _burden_ : a specific amount to be paid
2 tax _____ : getting taxes back
3 tax _____ : declaration of income
4 tax _____ : an increase in taxes
5 tax _____ : a decrease in taxes
6 tax _____ : an item which can lower your tax burden, e.g. a tax-free amount
7 tax _____ : benefit granted to encourage investments
8 tax _____ : an expense that reduces your taxable income
9 tax _____ : formal determination of tax burden
10 tax _____ : a range of income taxed at the same rate; also a class or category that depends on your family status

7 Listen to a dialogue between Jane Croud, a retired UK national living in Germany, and Martin Schmidt, a professional German tax advisor. Complete the table with phrases used in the dialogue.

> **VOCABULARY**
>
> **allowance** *hier:* Freibetrag
> **care insurance** Pflegeversicherung
> **contribution** Beitrag
> to **exceed sth** etw. überschreiten
> **income**-related **expenses** Werbungskosten
> **special expenses** Sonderausgaben

Meeting & greeting	Offering hospitality	Small talk

What other phrases do you know? Add them to the table and compare with a partner. Then read through the Useful Phrases on the next page.

USEFUL PHRASES — Meeting for the first time

Meeting & greeting

- Good morning, Mr Smith. How are you?
- I'm Klaus Müller. Nice to meet you.
- My name is Agata Beres. Pleased to meet you.
- This is my assistant, Sumiko Ito.
- May I introduce you to my partner in this firm, Mr Wang?

"How do you do?" is a formal, rather old-fashioned greeting. It is not a question. Do not answer it by saying that you are fine. Just say "How do you do?" as well.

Offering hospitality

- Would you like something to drink?
- Can I offer you a cup of coffee?
- May I offer you a glass of water?
- Please help yourself to milk and sugar.

Don't offer a drink as this usually means alcohol.

Small talk

- How was your journey/flight?
- How do you like your hotel?
- Did you find us alright? / Did you have any trouble finding us?
- Is this your first time in Germany? / Is this your first visit to Berlin?
- Terrible weather today, isn't it?

Good small-talk topics are travelling, accommodation, weather and sports. Personal and potentially sensitive issues, such as politics and religion, should be avoided.

8 Work with a partner and practise short conversations. Take turns to be the tax advisor and the client.

- Welcome the client to your firm.
- Guide him/her to the meeting room and make some small talk.
- Offer a seat and refreshments.

9 What phrase does Jane Croud use to move from small talk to business?

Come up with other phrases that can be used to move from small talk to business. Then share them with your partner.

10 Read an excerpt from an article on Certified Public Accountants (CPAs) in the USA.

The primary functions CPAs fulfill relate to assurance services, or public accounting. In assurance services, also known as financial audit services, CPAs attest to the reasonableness of disclosures, the freedom from material misstatement, and the adherence to the applicable generally accepted accounting principles (GAAP) in financial statements.

Although some CPAs serve as business consultants, the consulting role has been under scrutiny following the corporate climate in the aftermath of the Enron scandal. This has resulted in divestitures in the consulting divisions by many accounting firms. This trend has since reversed. In audit engagements, CPAs are required by professional standards and Federal and State laws to maintain independence from the entity for which they are conducting an attestation engagement. However, most individual CPAs who work as consultants do not work as auditors, or vice versa.

CPAs also have a niche within the income tax preparation industry. Many small to mid-sized firms have both a tax and an auditing department.

Whether providing services directly to the public or employed by corporations or associations, CPAs can operate in virtually any area of finance including:

- Assurance and Attestation Services
- Corporate Finance (Merger & Acquisition, initial public offerings, share & debt issuings)
- Corporate Governance
- Estate Planning
- Financial Accounting
- Financial Analysis
- Financial Planning
- Forensic Accounting (preventing, detecting, and investigating financial frauds)
- Income Tax
- Information Technology, especially as applied to accounting and auditing
- Management Consulting and Performance Management
- Tax Preparation and Planning
- Venture Capital

In order to become a U.S. CPA, the candidate must sit for and pass the Uniform Certified Public Accountant Examination (Uniform CPA Exam), which is set by the American Institute of Certified Public Accountants and administered by the National Association of State Boards of Accountancy.

Eligibility to sit for the Uniform CPA Exam is determined by individual State Boards of Accountancy. Typically the requirement is a U.S. bachelors degree which includes a minimum number of qualifying credit hours in accounting and business administration with an additional 1 year study. This requirement for 5 years study is known as the "150 hour rule". It has been adopted by 45 states.

The Uniform CPA exam tests general principles of state law such as the law of contracts and agency (questions not tailored to the variances of any particular state) and some federal law as well. Over 40 of the state boards now require applicants for CPA status to complete a special examination on ethics.

VOCABULARY

attestation Testat
divestiture Entflechtung
estate planning Nachfolgeplanung
forensic accounting forensische Wirtschaftsprüfung
material *hier:* wesentlich
reasonableness Angemessenheit
scrutiny Prüfung, Untersuchung

a **Mark the correct sentences.**

1. You must study business administration to become a CPA.
   You must take the Uniform CPA Exam to become a CPA.

2. CPAs may not provide consulting and auditing services to the same client.
   CPAs may provide consulting and auditing services to the same client.

3. Public accounting is also known as accounting services.
   Public accounting is also known as assurance services.

4. CPAs do not deal with taxes.
   CPAs also deal with taxes.

5. In most states, CPAs must take a special exam on ethics.
   In most states, CPAs must make a declaration on ethics.

b **Complete the diagram on the following presentation slide.**

Functions of CPAs

1. Assurance services = public _____ ¹

   = financial _____ ² services

   Attestation of:
   - reasonableness of disclosures
   - _____ ³ from misstatement
   - _____ ⁴ to GAAP

2. Consultancy

3. Income tax _____ ⁵

c **Match the items. Then explain them to your partner.**

1. assurance and attestation   a accounting
2. income   b consulting
3. corporate   c capital
4. estate   d finance
5. financial   e management
6. management   f planning
7. performance   g services
8. venture   h tax

d **Discuss the following questions.**

1. The article mentions "forensic accounting"? What is this?
2. What does the principle of maintaining independence entail?
3. What do you know about the Enron scandal and how it affected the accounting industry?

UNIT 1: INTRODUCTION TO TAXATION & AUDITING   11

11 MEDIATION

There are many jobs in accounting, and there is an abundance of German job titles and qualifications. Using the following article, compile an overview that explains these to an English-speaking client. Then compare it in a group.

While mediating, concentrate on keywords and paraphrasing rather than translating a text word by word.

Die Welt der Buchhalter

Viele Fachleute tummeln sich in den Bereichen Buchhaltung und Steuern. Was genau tun sie?

Ein **Buchhalter** kümmert sich um Zahlungen, dokumentiert Ein- und Ausgänge. Der Begriff ist nicht geschützt. Die Tätigkeit kann jedermann ausführen und durch praktische Tätigkeit erlernen. Häufig haben Buchhalter eine kaufmännische Ausbildung.

Ein **Lohnbuchhalter** wird überall dort benötigt, wo Mitarbeiter beschäftigt werden. Zu seinen Aufgaben gehören das das Erfassen und Pflegen von Daten, das Erstellen von Lohnabrechnungen und Meldungen an Finanzämter, Krankenkassen und Sozialversicherungsträger.

Bilanzbuchhalter kennen sich mit Rechnungslegungsvorschriften aus und erstellen Jahresabschlüsse und Steuererklärungen. Sie haben eine Prüfung abgelegt, die eine Berufsausbildung oder ein Studium sowie mehrjährige Berufserfahrung voraussetzt. Eine Steigerung ist die Prüfung zum **Internationalen Bilanzbuchhalter**, mit der Kenntnisse der europäischen Rechnungslegungsvorschriften und der Bilanzierung nach IFRS nachgewiesen werden.

Debitorenbuchhalter kümmern sich um das Forderungsmanagement ihres Unternehmens, überwachen Zahlungseingänge und veranlassen Mahnungen. Ihnen stehen **Kreditorenbuchhalter** gegenüber. Sie kümmern sich um Zahlungspflichten und sorgen für eine fristgerechte Begleichung von erhaltenen Rechnungen.

Finanzbuchhalter haben ein weites Tätigkeitsfeld und kümmern sich um das Kontieren von Belegen, verwalten Konten und überprüfen Gewinn- oder Verlustrechnungen. Sie können auch Bilanzen erstellen, sich um Finanzierungen kümmern und haben das große Ganze im Blick. Auch hier handelt es sich um eine Fortbildung, die man absolvieren kann, um als Finanzbuchhalter tätig zu sein.

Controller sind für die Planung, Steuerung und Kontrolle eines Unternehmens zuständig. Sie versorgen das Management mit entscheidungsrelevanten Informationen und helfen bei der Umsetzung von Maßnahmen. Sie verwalten Budgets, analysieren Märkte und Risiken, und haben eine herausragende Stellung bei der gewinnorientierten Tätigkeit ihres Unternehmens.

Steuerfachangestellte haben eine mehrjährige Ausbildung durchlaufen und sind die „rechte Hand" des Steuerberaters. Sie bereiten Steuererklärungen aller Art vor und korrespondieren mit Ämtern und Mandanten, führen Akten, pflegen Terminkalender und überwachen Fristen. Sie können sich zum **Steuerfachwirt** fortbilden und vertiefte Kenntnisse im Steuerrecht, wie auch Grundzüge der Betriebswirtschaft und des Wirtschaftsrechts, erwerben. Eine Fachkraft mit Führungsaufgaben und erweiterten Tätigkeits- und Verantwortungsbereich.

OVER TO YOU

The accountancy profession in the UK and the US

There are six professional accounting bodies in the UK and the Republic of Ireland, with more than half a million members. The largest is the **Institute of Chartered Accountants in England and Wales (ICAEW)**, which has around 150,000 members.

Individuals who operate in the areas of audit and insolvency must be registered, and only members of certain accountancy bodies are eligible for such registration. Likewise individuals who describe themselves as "chartered accountants" must be a member of an accountancy body, and if working in public practice these chartered accountants must comply with additional regulations such as holding indemnity insurance and submitting to regular and independent inspections.

Accounting bodies operate disciplinary procedures to deal with professional conduct matters. They can reprimand or even exclude members, impose fines and make orders to compensate people who made a complaint. Among the private-sector accounting firms, the Big Four have a market share of 80%.

The **American Institute of Certified Public Accountants (AICPA)** is the national professional organization of Certified Public Accountants (CPAs) in the United States, with more than 428,000 members. AICPA sets generally accepted professional and technical standards in multiple areas, including auditing and ethics. They also develop and grade the Uniform CPA Examination, which everybody who wants to be licensed must pass. Members must attest to meeting the requirements for their membership every year, complying with the AICPA's bylaws and its Code of Profession Conduct. Members are subject to audit and, if found to be non-compliant, may be expelled from the institute.

Common reasons for losing a CPA licence include non-renewal, attestation services under an unlicensed firm, continued use of the CPA title after expiry, misrepresenting completion of the continuing education requirements, and a number of "discreditable acts", such as not following applicable auditing standards or committing crimes. 80% of the US market is shared among the Big Four.

VOCABULARY

conduct (*hier:* berufsrechtlich relevantes) Handeln, Verhalten
discreditable unrühmlich
eligible berechtigt
expiry Ablauf
indemnity insurance Berufshaftpflichtversicherung
to reprimand so jmdn. verwarnen

1 Is there an equivalent body in your country? What are its functions?
2 Who are the "Big Four"? Have they always been four?
3 Do they have a similar market share in your country? Who is the biggest?

IN THIS UNIT YOU WILL …
- discuss personal taxation
- conduct client interviews
- write client briefs

2 Advising employees

What types of income do you distinguish? Fill in the missing letters.

1 farmi_g & for_stry
2 tr_de
3 se_f-em_loyment
4 em_lo_ment
5 cap_tal ass_ts
6 re_t_l
7 _ther

What type of income do the following situations belong to?
Write numbers 1–6 from above in each box.

- a dividend payments
- b wages & salaries
- c leasing a flat to someone
- d being a freelance teacher
- e pensions
- f being a freelance craftsman
- g interest payments
- h being a freelance translator
- i running a grocery store
- j being a freelance real estate agent

 1 Match the following taxes with their German equivalents. Indicate in the right column which taxes employees are usually (+), possibly (~), or not (−) subjected to. Work with a partner and discuss why.

1 value-added tax (VAT)	a Gewerbesteuer	
2 insurance tax	b Grunderwerbsteuer	
3 wage tax	c Umsatzsteuer	
4 capital gains tax	d Solidaritätszuschlag	
5 inheritance tax	e Körperschaftsteuer	
6 church tax	f Versicherungsteuer	
7 trade tax	g Lohnsteuer	
8 solidarity tax	h Erbschaftsteuer	
9 corporation tax	i Abgeltungsteuer	
10 real estate transfer tax	j Kirchensteuer	

2 John Blair is calling the office of Thomas Meister, a German tax firm based in Düsseldorf.
Listen and tick the sentences you hear.

1. ☐ How can I help you?
   ☐ What can I do for you?
2. ☐ I'll just check the diary. Please hold.
   ☐ Let me just check the diary. Please hold the line.
3. ☐ Would Wednesday at 9 o'clock be convenient?
   ☐ Would Wednesday at 9 o'clock suit you?
4. ☐ I've scheduled you for Wednesday at 9 o'clock. Mr Meister will take care of you.
   ☐ I've entered you for Wednesday at 9 o'clock. Mr Meister will see you.
5. ☐ The fee for an initial consultation is € 150.
   ☐ We usually charge € 150 plus VAT for an initial consultation.

> **VOCABULARY**
>
> **initial consultation** Erstberatung
> **to schedule so/sth** jmdn./etw. einplanen, (terminlich) eintragen
> **to suit so** jmdm. passen

Listen again and answer the following questions.

1. What is the reason for the call? _____
2. What is John's phone number? _____
3. What is the website's address where John can find directions?
   _____

USEFUL PHRASES   Giving short answers

Question	Short answer
1. Sorry, do you speak English?	– Certainly. What can I do for you?
2. Can I just read that back to you: …	– That's correct.
3. Would Wednesday at 9 o'clock suit you?	– Unfortunately, it doesn't. How about …?
4. May I have your phone number?	– Of course, it's …
5. Is that acceptable to you?	– I think so.

Another option is to use *yes* or *no* with one of the above, or with an auxiliary verb.

1. Have you already been assigned a tax number?	– Yes, I have.
2. Did you have a tax advisor in the past?	– No, I didn't.
3. Will you ask your employer?	– Yes, I will.

Do not get confused and pay attention to how the question is put forward:
- Do you have a car? → Yes, I ~~have~~ do.
- Have you got a car? → Yes, I have.

> *When answering questions, you can give **short answers**. However, just saying "yes" and "no" is not the best way to do this. This can sound abrupt, even rude. Use linking words to make the transitions smoother.*

3 Practise giving short answers.
What sort of questions do you ask when you collect information from clients?
Ask and answer with a partner.

UNIT 2: ADVISING EMPLOYEES   15

4 John Blair has arrived for his meeting with Thomas Meister. Read the beginning of their conversation. How would you answer his question?

Thomas: Please have a seat. What can I do for you, Mr Blair?
John: Well, I've recently moved from England to Germany. I'll start a full-time job in the export department of a local company next month, and I'd like to get some information on taxes here. It was a nightmare getting my papers, because everything has become so complicated after Brexit. But I'm all set now.
Thomas: I'm sorry to hear that. What exactly would you like to know?
John: Well, first of all, I'd like to learn something about deductions. I'll earn € 3,000 a month, and I was wondering how much I'll have in my bank account at the end of the day.

5 Listen to the second part and complete the exercises that follow.

> **VOCABULARY**
>
> **deductions** Abzüge
> **incentive** Anreiz
> to **levy sth** etw. erheben
> to **opt for sth** sich für etw. entscheiden
> **source** Quelle
> **surcharge** Zuschlag, Zusatzbeitrag
> **threshold** Grenze
> **tier** Stufe
> **uniform rate** einheitlicher Satz

a What do the following numbers refer to?

- 20 _____
- 40 _____
- 1200 _____
- 1800 _____
- 12 000 _____
- 15 000 _____
- 36 000 _____

b Complete the sentences with expressions from the dialogue.

1 Taxes _____ your income and family situation.
2 Employers _____ taxes on income _____ € 15,000.
3 Certain _____ are automatically taken into account.
4 You can _____ to pay about 20% income tax.
5 Do I have to _____ a tax return?
6 You'll get a _____ with a _____ number.
7 Filing a return could be advisable as you often get a _____ .

c Are the following statements true or false?   True   False

1 Taxes on John's income will be deducted by his employer.
2 Pension contributions will be shared equally between John and his employer.
3 John has the opportunity to take out private health insurance.
4 State health insurance costs the same everywhere.
5 John is advised to file a tax return, but he does not have to.

d What are the four pillars of social security?

_____

Strictly speaking, there is a fifth pillar only employers pay for. Which one? What is it for?

USEFUL PHRASES Conducting client interviews & giving advice

Giving advice
- must — You **must** file your tax return by 31 May.
- have to — You **have to** enclose receipts.
- ought to — You **ought to** do it electronically.
- should — You **should** consider paying later.
- suggest — I (would) **suggest** calling your tax officer.
  I (would) **suggest** that I write to your tax office.
- recommend — I (would) **recommend** filing an appeal.
  I (would) **recommend** that you do not react.

*Client interviews can be very demanding. The structure of such interviews is reflected in the **WASP approach**:*
→ *Welcome the client*
→ *Acquire information*
→ *Supply information and advise*
→ *Part (say goodbye)*

In the examples above, *would* makes the sentence more formal and polite.

*Switching between **levels of formality** is an essential skill when dealing with clients. Formal language helps to build a professional and focused atmosphere when eliciting information, giving advice, and explaining.*

Being more and less informal

Formal
- I would advise you to accept the decision.
- I recommend that you pay the penalty.
- Perhaps you could talk to your employer.
- I suggest that you get a confirmation from your payroll department.
- I think you'd better clarify your status.

Informal
- I'd accept it.
- I think you should pay the penalty.
- Why don't you talk to your boss?
- If I were you, I'd get a confirmation from the people in payroll.
- You should clarify this!

6 SIMULATION

Conduct client interviews with other members of your group and discuss topics particularly relevant for employees. Pick 3 topics you often deal with in your own practice and write each topic on the top line of the table. Then add keywords reflecting the issues you need to address.

topic: working from home	topic:	topic:	topic:
requirements			
allowance			
limitations			

With other members of your group, take turns addressing the first topic on your list. Give advice as if in a client interview using the WASP approach and the Useful Phrases. Do two more rounds for topics two and three.

UNIT 2: ADVISING EMPLOYEES

7 Read about the zero conditional. Then use it to translate the sentences below.

> **Zero conditional**
>
> When explaining rules and giving advice, you often express conditions. Conditional sentences consist of a main clause and a conditional clause (also called if-clause). The conditional clause usually begins with *if* or *unless*, and it can come before or after the main clause. Most people have heard about **three types of conditionals**:
>
> **1** If you file a tax return, you will get a refund. ← possible
> **2** If you filed a tax return, you would get a refund. ← theoretically possible
> **3** If you had filed a tax return, you would have got a refund. ← impossible
>
> What you often do not hear about is a **fourth type** that is particularly relevant for consultants: the **zero conditional**. It uses the simple present in both the if- and the main clause. It is used to refer to facts or universal truths:
> You **do not have to** *file a tax return if you* **earn** *nothing but wages.*
>
> As you regularly explain laws and regulations (=facts/truths), you can often rely on this simple conditional.
>
> **Note:** No comma when the main clause comes first.

1 Sie sind zur Abgabe einer Steuererklärung verpflichtet, wenn Sie Einkünfte aus selbständiger Arbeit erzielen.
2 Wenn Sie Zinsen von Ihrer Bank erhalten, fällt Abgeltungsteuer an.
3 Wenn Ihre Werbungskosten gering sind, berücksichtigt das Finanzamt automatisch den höheren Arbeitnehmerpauschbetrag.
4 Sie können innerhalb eines Monats Einspruch einlegen, wenn Sie mit einem Steuerbescheid nicht einverstanden sind.
5 Wenn Sie einen Nebenjob aufnehmen, wird dieser nach Steuerklasse 6 besteuert.

> **VOCABULARY**
>
> **capital gains tax, flat-rate withholding tax** Abgeltungssteuer
> **employee allowance, employee standard deduction** Arbeitnehmerpauschbetrag
> to **file an appeal**, to **appeal** Einspruch einlegen
> **tax (assessment) notice** Steuerbescheid
> **tax bracket, filing status (AE)** Steuerklasse

8 Discuss the following allowances employees can benefit from. Explain what they are for and give their current amounts. Can you add any other?

- Arbeitnehmerpauschbetrag
- Pendlerpauschale
- Homeoffice-Pauschale
- Sparerfreibetrag
- _____

9 Who is the odd one out? In each line, cross out the word that doesn't fit.

clothing	~~cash~~	computer	goods
social security	health insurance	car insurance	pension insurance
return	refund	reimbursement	repayment
expenses	costs	disbursements	claims
tax	salary	wage	remuneration
married	alone	divorced	widowed
keep	retain	withdraw	withhold

ENGLISH FOR TAX PROFESSIONALS

> **DID YOU KNOW?**
>
> **Remote work** has become quite common during the pandemic, and many people have discovered the benefits of working from home. They have more flexibility, freedom and time, save travelling and costs – and stay safe. After the pandemic, quite a few employees have found arrangements with their employers to continue working in this way, at least for a certain number of days per week or month. However, nobody does that in, at or from their home office as nobody has a *home office* at home! This phrase is "Denglisch" and fuelled by widespread uses in business (*Homeoffice*) and in tax law (*Homeoffice-Pauschale*). In the UK, the Home Office is the interior ministry and has a Home Secretary (*Innenminister*in*). In the US, it is another word for a company's head office or headquarters.
>
> Use **study (room)** or simply **working from home** instead. In emails and text messages, some people even use the acronym *WFH*:
> - *I'll be working from home tomorrow.*
> - *WFH tomorrow!*

10 Drafting a memorandum

A while after John Blair started working, he sends this email to Thomas Meister.

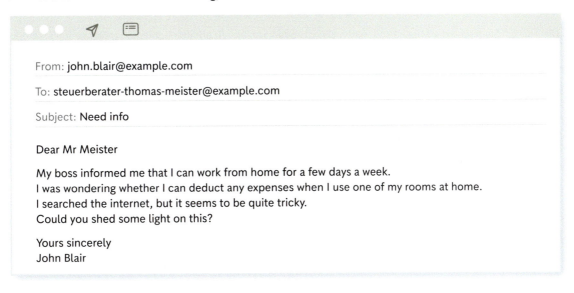

From: john.blair@example.com

To: steuerberater-thomas-meister@example.com

Subject: **Need info**

Dear Mr Meister

My boss informed me that I can work from home for a few days a week.
I was wondering whether I can deduct any expenses when I use one of my rooms at home.
I searched the internet, but it seems to be quite tricky.
Could you shed some light on this?

Yours sincerely
John Blair

As remote work is a topic that comes up again and again in his practice, Thomas would like to prepare a client brief he can use and hand out if the need arises. This will save him a lot of work and time.

a **Draft a text of not more than 300 words, explaining the tax implications of working from home. Cover requirements, amounts and pitfalls. Consider visualizing your explanations by using a table, diagram or other means.**

b **Present and discuss your findings in class.**

c **Draft an email forwarding the brief you prepared. Use the Useful Phrases from page 33 and the phrases on pages 72 and 73 to help you.**

UNIT 2: ADVISING EMPLOYEES | 19

DID YOU KNOW?

Income is not just money. An employer can also provide a number of **additional benefits**, such as a company car, a flat, catering, free or discounted goods and services. Such non-cash benefits are called **"perks"**, **"fringe benefits"** or **"benefits in-kind"** (*Sachbezug, geldwerter Vorteil*). They count as income and are therefore taxable. Thus, they are best translated as **"taxable benefits"** to convey that meaning. There are certain tax-free allowances and average rates employers and employees can take advantage of. Goods and services are tax free up to a value of € 50 per month, and favourable amounts apply above that. For example, breakfast is taxed at € 2, lunch and dinner at € 3.80 each. They probably cost more. Bon appetit!

 11 MEDIATION

John Blair has forwarded a memo he received from his employer and asks you to explain it. Draft a client email outlining the tax implications addressed. Include a sample tax calculation for a car with a list price of € 50,000 gross, assuming a travel distance to work of 10 km.

p. 72

Sie haben die Möglichkeit, einen Dienstwagen von uns zu erhalten, der auch privat genutzt werden kann. Bitte beachten Sie dabei, dass dies einen sog. "geldwerten Vorteil" darstellt, der versteuert werden muss. Hierfür gibt es verschiedene Methoden: eine Pauschalversteuerung nach der sog. 1%-Methode, bei welcher der Wert des Pkw anhand des Bruttolistenpreises herangezogen wird, zuzüglich des Weges zur Arbeit, d.h. der Entfernung zwischen Ihrer Wohn- und Arbeitsstätte. Alternativ können Sie den tatsächlichen privaten Nutzungsanteil anhand eines Fahrtenbuchs ermitteln.
Zu den Einzelheiten lassen Sie sich bitte fachkundig beraten.
Bitte melden Sie sich bei der Personalabteilung, wenn Sie von unserem Angebot Gebrauch machen möchten.

 12 Discuss the pros & cons of both methods. When would you advise using which method?

13 Complete the crossword.

1 a limit, cap or ceiling
2 getting a tax ...
3 money paid in compensation for performed work
4 the official notice you get from your tax office
5 when income is taxed at the same rate, it falls into the same tax ...
6 a remedy you have when you are unhappy with an official decision
7 extra pay
8 a record of travels with your company car
9 filing a tax ...
10 wages are processed by ... accounting

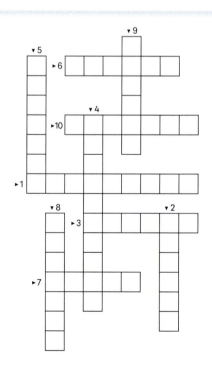

OVER TO YOU

Taxes in the UK & the US

In the **United Kingdom**, income is taxed using a number of bands. There are only three rates. The table shows the tax rates you pay in each band in England, Wales and Northern Ireland. Slightly different bands and rates apply to Scotland.

Band	Taxable income	Tax rate
Personal Allowance	Up to £ 12,570	0%
Basic rate	£ 12,571 to £ 50,270	20%
Higher rate	£ 50,271 to £ 125,140	40%
Additional rate	over £ 125,140	45%

You may be able to take advantage of an allowance if you are married. This is an amount of up to £ 1,260 provided that one of you stays below the personal allowance. You can then transfer the amount to the partner who earns more, thus reducing the taxable income.

In the **United States**, income tax rates and brackets for single taxpayers look like this:

Taxable income (USD)	Tax rate (%)
0 to 11,000	10
11,001–44,725	12
44,726–95,375	22
95,376–182,100	24
182,101–231,250	32
231,251–578,125	35
578,126+	37

Other bands apply to married taxpayers filing jointly. Most states, and a number of municipal authorities, impose some personal income tax on individuals working or residing in their area, applying either a flat or a progressive rate. These rates vary between 0.25% and 10.9%, with Delaware, Mississippi and South Carolina at the bottom, and New York at the top end of the scale. Alaska, Florida, Nevada, New Hampshire, South Dakota, Texas, Tennessee, Washington and Wyoming impose no personal income tax.

(Figures for 2024)

1. How does income tax in the UK and the US compare with its treatment in your own country?
2. Are there similarities or significant differences?
3. Do individuals pay any local taxes?

VOCABULARY

band *hier:* Tarifstufe
jointly gemeinsam
municipal authority Gemeindeverwaltung
personal allowance Grundfreibetrag

IN THIS UNIT YOU WILL ...
- hold a meeting to discuss freelancer issues
- explain tax forms
- discuss accounting

3 Advising freelancers

 What do you know about self-employment? Discuss the following questions.

1. What are the advantages & disadvantages of being self-employed?
2. What are examples of typical self-employed professions?
3. Assuming the people in the pictures below are self-employed, are they treated the same tax-wise? Do they use the same tax forms? Why (not)?
4. What happens if someone pursues multiple professions that fall into different categories, e.g. a journalist also working as a real-estate agent?
5. Are the different regulations justified from a professional, social and tax point of view?

> **DID YOU KNOW?**
>
> The English term **freelancer** refers to anybody who is self-employed and should therefore not be confused with the German *Freiberufler*in*, which is a narrow concept of referring to people performing scientific, artistic, authorial, teaching or educational work. Examples include musicians, painters, journalists, writers, teachers and translators, but also doctors and dentists, architects, lawyers, tax advisors and auditors. Their treatment differs from that of other self-employed people classified as **traders** (*Gewerbetreibende*), who are subject to trade tax and have more registration and reporting requirements (even separate tax forms). Since the word freelancer does not reflect such a distinction, it is better to refer to **professionals** or **professional services** when having the German *Freie Berufe* in mind.

ENGLISH FOR TAX PROFESSIONALS

1 Three years after coming to Germany, British national John Blair is at another meeting with German tax advisor Thomas Meister. Listen to their dialogue. Then complete the exercises that follow.

05

> **VOCABULARY**
>
> to **assign sth** etw. zuweisen
> **demand** Nachfrage
> to **incur sth** etw. verursachen
> **transitory item** durchlaufender Posten
> **turnover** Umsatz

a Match the following terms from the dialogue with their definitions.

1 turnover
2 deduction
3 transitory item
4 burden
5 fraction

a what you have to pay or are subject to
b a part of an amount
c when you subtract something
d the total amount of income before any deductions (BE)
e a position that does not affect your income as it does not stay with you permanently

b Replace the underlined words with words from the box.

> account for | additional | apartment | commission | costs | decrease |
> forward | hours | irrespective | meet (2x) | revenue | subtract

1 My employer is going to reduce my <u>workload</u> (_____).

2 I'd like to earn some <u>extra</u> (_____) money to make up for the lost income.

3 I've already talked to a few language schools, and they would be happy to <u>hire</u> (_____) me.

4 Then you'll have to prepare invoices that <u>match</u> (_____) certain criteria.

5 Will I have to <u>charge</u> (_____) VAT?

6 If your <u>turnover</u> (_____) exceeds €22,000, you'll have to charge it. But you can opt for charging it anyway, <u>independent</u> (_____) of your turnover.

7 The advantage of charging VAT is that you can <u>deduct</u> (_____) the VAT you pay on goods and services bought for your business from your VAT burden.

8 So it certainly is advantageous when you incur significant <u>expenses</u> (_____), for example a car, office space rent and equipment.

9 You'll <u>pass on</u> (_____) the VAT you collect to your tax office on a monthly or quarterly basis.

10 It's basically to make up for the lost hours and the salary <u>cut</u> (_____) involved.

11 Can I actually deduct the rent I pay for my <u>flat</u> (_____)?

12 Are there any deadlines to <u>observe</u> (_____)?

c In the dialogue, Thomas Meister promised to send John Blair details about invoicing. Draft a list with keywords and a sample invoice showing the legal requirements.

UNIT 3: ADVISING FREELANCERS   23

> **USEFUL PHRASES**
>
> **Signposting**
>
> - **First of all**, let us think about …
> - **Then**, we need to …
> - **Next**, you have to decide …
> - **Finally**, we have to complete …
> - **Let's start with** item three.
> - **Let's look at** page four.
> - **Let's move on to** section five.

*When giving a presentation or when explaining different steps in a process, e.g. discussing a business plan or explaining a start-up process, **sequencing language** helps in structuring your talk.*

2 SIMULATION

Have a meeting to discuss what issues can arise when advising freelancers. Each come up with three questions your clients (professionals/traders) typically have in regard to starting and running their business. Then discuss these questions, giving essential information on setting up a business, registration and reporting requirements as well as taxes.

	Professionals	Traders
Starting		
Running		

3 A few months later, John Blair and Thomas Meister are having a video call to go through the form that has to be submitted in connection with John's freelance work. Listen to the dialogue and complete the form on the next page.

*Most tax forms in Germany are named "**Anlage XYZ**" as they supplement the main form. This might be "annex" or "appendix" in English, but you can simply refer to them as "**Form XYZ**".*

> **VOCABULARY**
>
> **cash accounting** Einnahmenüberschuss-rechnung
> **column** Spalte
> to **estimate sth** etw. schätzen
> **small entrepreneur** Kleinunternehmer
> to **submit sth** etw. übermitteln, einreichen

ENGLISH FOR TAX PROFESSIONALS

Fragebogen zur steuerlichen Erfassung

☐ Aufnahme einer gewerblichen, selbständigen (freiberuflichen) oder land- und forstwirtschaftlichen Tätigkeit

3. Angaben zur Festsetzung der Vorauszahlungen (Einkommensteuer, Gewerbesteuer)

3.1 Voraussichtliche Einkünfte aus	im Jahr der Betriebseröffnung		im Folgejahr	
	Steuerpflichtige(r) EUR	Ehegatte(in)/ Lebenspartner(in) EUR	Steuerpflichtige(r) EUR	Ehegatte(in)/ Lebenspartner(in) EUR
Land- und Forstwirtschaft				
Gewerbebetrieb				
Selbständiger Arbeit				
Nichtselbständiger Arbeit				
Kapitalvermögen				
Vermietung und Verpachtung				
Sonstigen Einkünften (z. B. Renten)				

4. Angaben zur Gewinnermittlung

Gewinnermittlungsart
1 = Einnahmenüberschussrechnung
2 = Betriebsvermögensvergleich
3 = Gewinnermittlung nach Durchschnittssätzen (nur bei Land- und Forstwirtschaft)
4 = Sonstige (z.B. § 5a EStG) *(Angaben bitte in Zusatzzeile vornehmen)*

Angaben zu Sonstige

Hinweis: Die Eröffnungsbilanz ist gemäß § 5b Abs. 1 Satz 5 EStG nach amtlich vorgeschriebenen Datensatz durch Datenfernübertragung zu übermitteln.

7. Angaben zur Anmeldung und Abführung der Umsatzsteuer

7.1 Summe der Umsätze (geschätzt)	im Jahr der Betriebseröffnung EUR	im Folgejahr EUR

7.3 Kleinunternehmer-Regelung

☐ Der auf das Kalenderjahr hochgerechnete Gesamtumsatz wird die Grenze des § 19 Abs. 1 UStG voraussichtlich nicht überschreiten. Es wird die Kleinunternehmer-Regelung in Anspruch genommen.

In Rechnungen wird keine Umsatzsteuer gesondert ausgewiesen und es kann kein Vorsteuerabzug geltend gemacht werden.

Hinweis: Angaben zu Tz. 7.8 sind nicht erforderlich; Umsatzsteuer-Voranmeldungen sind grundsätzlich nicht zu übermitteln.

☐ Der auf das Kalenderjahr hochgerechnete Gesamtumsatz wird die Grenze des § 19 Abs. 1 UStG voraussichtlich nicht überschreiten. Es wird auf die Anwendung der Kleinunternehmer-Regelung verzichtet.

Die Besteuerung erfolgt nach den allgemeinen Vorschriften des Umsatzsteuergesetzes **für mindestens fünf Kalenderjahre** (§ 19 Abs. 2 UStG); Umsatzsteuer-Voranmeldungen sind monatlich in elektronischer Form authentifiziert zu übermitteln.

7.8 Soll-/Istversteuerung der Entgelte

Ich berechne die Umsatzsteuer nach ☐ vereinbarten Entgelten (**Sollversteuerung**).

oder

☐ vereinnahmten Entgelten. Ich beantrage hiermit die **Istversteuerung**, weil

☐ der auf das Kalenderjahr hochgerechnete Gesamtumsatz für das Gründungsjahr voraussichtlich nicht mehr als 500.000 EUR betragen wird.

☐ ich von der Verpflichtung, Bücher zu führen und auf Grund jährlicher Bestandsaufnahmen regelmäßig Abschlüsse zu machen, nach § 148 Abgabenordnung (AO) befreit bin.

☐ ich Umsätze ausführe, für die ich als Angehöriger eines freien Berufs im Sinne von § 18 Abs. 1 Nr. 1 des Einkommensteuergesetzes weder buchführungspflichtig bin noch freiwillig Bücher führe.

4 Are the following statements true or false? True False

1 John has to indicate the turnover he expects to make.
2 John has to indicate the profit he expects to make.
3 The figures he has to estimate are for a three-year period.
4 John has to draft a proper balance sheet.

UNIT 3: ADVISING FREELANCERS

> **DID YOU KNOW?**
>
> There is widespread uncertainty about the differences between **turnover, revenue, sales** and **income**. For the layperson, these terms are often the same and refer to money received. In business, and then again in Europe and the US, there are differences.
> **"Revenue"** is a US term for the amount of money a company receives. In Europe, and especially in the UK, the equivalent term is **"turnover"**. However, under IFRS terminology (International Financial Reporting Standards), revenue is used as an income statement item. The official translation is *Umsatzerlöse*. On the other hand, in the US, turnover refers to changes in inventory, i.e. how often an item is sold and replaced in the course of business. It can also refer to staff, i.e. the number or percentage of employees who joined and left a company in a given period.
> **Sales** is revenue or turnover generated from selling goods or services, and is therefore narrower (unless this is the only type of income the company makes). **Income** is a general term mostly used by and for individuals. Yet you may hear accountants using the term "net income" when referring to profits. Taxes and fees states collect are often referred to as "government revenues".

5 A few months have passed, and John Blair sends a follow-up email. Read the email and draft a reply.

p. 72

Dear Mr Meister

I've started teaching at two private language schools. Eight hours per week. I really enjoy it.
I might be able to get some direct clients, too.
As far as accounting is concerned, could you give me an overview of what I can deduct in the end?
I was thinking of travel costs I have (I'm going by car), as well as books and teaching aids I buy.
A colleague also told me that treating my students to lunch is tax-deductible. I'd also like to give everyone my favourite Harry Potter book at the end. Your advice is much appreciated.

Kind regards
John Blair

6 Discuss these scenarios in terms of their tax deductibility.

a John pays an annual bank account maintenance fee of € 80.
b He has been commissioned to give a two-day workshop in Berlin.
c He attends a teachers' conference in Brighton.
d He buys an e-scooter and uses it for travelling to work.
e He joins a sports club and a teachers' association.
f He takes out personal liability, professional indemnity and occupational disability insurance.

VOCABULARY

occupational disability insurance
  Berufsunfähigkeitsversicherung
personal liability insurance
  Privathaftpflichtversicherung
professional indemnity insurance
  Berufshaftpflichtversicherung

p. 54

7 Freelancers who do cash accounting in Germany are required to complete a special form *(Anlage EÜR)*. Look at the expenses part of that form and explain where the above costs are to be entered. Discuss additional items that could be relevant for John Blair.

*It is also possible to say "private" instead of "personal", and "liability" instead of "indemnity". Other **key insurance terms** include: beneficiary (Begünstigte*r) | cover (Deckungssumme) | deductible (Selbstbeteiligung) | insured person | insurer | policy | policyholder (Versicherungsnehmer*in)*

8 Add the English equivalents to the following items from *Anlage EÜR*.

debt interest | depreciation | entertainment expenses | gifts | intangible assets | maintenance costs | meal allowance | reserves | small-value items | study

1 Geschenke:
2 Häusliches Arbeitszimmer:
3 Rücklagen:
4 Absetzung für Abnutzung:
5 immaterielle Wirtschaftsgüter:
6 geringwertige Wirtschaftsgüter:
7 Erhaltungsaufwendungen:
8 Schuldzinsen:
9 Bewirtungsaufwendungen:
10 Verpflegungsmehraufwendungen:

9 Read the following text. Use another form of the word in bold on the right (verb, adjective, etc.) that fits correctly in the structure of the text. Write the words on the lines to the right.

Deducting things you buy for work

Usually you cannot *deduct*¹ items all at once. You have to include them in a dedicated list and depreciate them over a number of years (their so-called [ ]² working life). There are tables provided by the government that tell you how long the depreciation period and the percentage per year for a specific item is. Laptops, for instance, must be [ ]³ over a period of three years, cars six years, and office furniture 13 years. To access the tables, simply search the internet for *AfA-Tabellen*. Two things are important:
- Depreciation follows the straight line method. This means you deduct the same amount every year. Some countries also apply a [ ]⁴ balance method.
- You must pro-rate the amount in the year you buy the item. If you buy it in July, you can only deduct 6/12 of the amount for that year.

Example: In July, you buy a photocopier for € 1,000. The depreciation period according to the [ ]⁵ table is seven years. Thus, the amount per year is € 142.86. In the year of purchase, you can only deduct € 71.43 (for the six months from July to December).

But there is [ ]⁶. Imagine you buy a desk for € 500. The money is spent, but you can only deduct € 38.46 per year over the next 13 years. Not nice. The answer is "small value item". You can deduct an item all in one go [ ]⁷ hat:
- costs no more than € 800 net.
- can be used on its own.

A chair, lamp, laptop computer, tablet or mobile phone can be used on its own. A printer, monitor or keyboard cannot. If you have a [ ]⁸ between buying a big bookshelf for € 1200 or three smaller ones for € 400 each, the smarter option is to go for the smaller ones and deduct the entire costs in that calendar year.

~~DEDUCTION~~
USE
_____ 2

DEPRECIATION
_____ 3

TO DECLINE
_____ 4

OFFICE
_____ 5

TO RELIEVE
_____ 6

PROVISION
_____ 7

TO CHOOSE
_____ 8

10 MEDIATION

Read the text and make a diagram presenting the information. Once finished, present the diagram to the class.

Aufwendungen für ein häusliches Arbeitszimmer sind grundsätzlich **nicht** abzugsfähig. Sie können nur dann abgezogen werden, wenn das Arbeitszimmer den **Mittelpunkt der gesamten Betätigung** bildet. Anstelle der tatsächlichen Aufwendungen kann auch eine Jahrespauschale in Höhe von 1.260 € abgezogen werden. Für jeden Kalendermonat, in dem die Voraussetzungen nicht vorliegen, ermäßigt sich diese um ein Zwölftel.

Ein häusliches Arbeitszimmer ist ein Raum, der seiner Lage, Funktion und Ausstattung nach in die häusliche Sphäre eingebunden ist, vorwiegend der Erledigung gedanklicher, schriftlicher, verwaltungstechnischer oder -organisatorischer Arbeiten dient und ausschließlich oder nahezu ausschließlich zu betrieblichen und/oder beruflichen Zwecken genutzt wird. Eine untergeordnete private Mitbenutzung (< 10 %) ist unschädlich. Ein Raum, der mit einem nicht unerheblichen Teil seiner Fläche auch privat genutzt wird (sog. „Arbeitsecke"), ist **kein** häusliches Arbeitszimmer und erlaubt keinen Abzug.

Beispiele für ein Arbeitszimmer:
- häusliches Büro eines selbständigen Handelsvertreters, eines selbständigen Übersetzers oder eines selbständigen Journalisten;
- ausschließlich betrieblich genutztes Musikzimmer einer freiberuflich tätigen Konzertpianistin, in dem diese Musikunterricht erteilt;
- ein Raum, in ein Telearbeitsplatz unterhalten wird, der dem Typus des häuslichen Arbeitszimmers entspricht.

Ein häusliches Arbeitszimmer bildet den Mittelpunkt der gesamten Betätigung, wenn nach Würdigung des Gesamtbildes der Verhältnisse und der Tätigkeitsmerkmale dort diejenigen Handlungen vorgenommen und Leistungen erbracht werden, die für die ausgeübte Tätigkeit **wesentlich** und **prägend** sind.

Bei Lehrern etwa befindet sich der Mittelpunkt der Betätigung regelmäßig nicht im häuslichen Arbeitszimmer, da das Unterrichten berufsprägend ist und in einer Schule oder einer anderen auswärtigen Einrichtung stattfindet. Ein Abzug von Aufwendungen kommt somit auch dann nicht in Betracht, wenn die überwiegende Arbeitszeit auf Unterrichtsvor- und -nachbereitung verwendet und diese Tätigkeit im häuslichen Arbeitszimmer ausgeübt wird.

11 Find 20 words from this unit in the grid. They are written horizontally, vertically, diagonally, backwards and forwards.

I	I	N	V	O	I	C	E	D	G	M	A
N	E	I	E	T	R	A	D	E	E	S	E
T	R	N	V	D	P	I	R	V	A	B	N
E	E	S	C	E	R	R	C	L	N	U	T
R	S	U	T	P	O	S	E	O	V	S	E
E	E	R	U	R	F	S	T	C	S	N	R
S	R	A	R	E	E	F	E	E	S	O	T
T	V	N	N	C	S	T	U	D	Y	I	A
R	E	C	O	I	S	L	N	S	F	S	I
A	S	E	V	A	I	L	M	O	G	I	N
V	E	N	E	T	O	I	R	D	I	V	M
E	U	I	R	I	N	P	O	O	F	O	E
L	L	I	B	O	A	V	F	S	T	R	N
V	A	T	C	N	L	A	R	S	I	P	T

28 ENGLISH FOR TAX PROFESSIONALS

OVER TO YOU

Welcome to Absurdville!

It seems to make sense: some things we need, some things we do not need. So let us make the things we really need cheaper than the rest! This is the idea behind different sales tax rates. But who decides what we "really" need? Is it food and beverages? Clothing? Computers?

Sales tax, also called value-added tax (VAT), is a tax charged on goods and services. Most countries in the world have it, and it is often their largest source of income. While it is a national tax in the UK, it is a state (and sometimes also a local) tax in the US with regional differences.

Many countries operate a system of different VAT rates: a standard rate, a reduced rate and a zero rate, distinguishing different goods and services. The standard rate in the UK is 20%, the reduced rate 5%. In Germany, 19% and 7% apply. But understanding what is charged at what rate and why is somewhat confusing.

7%	19%
apples	apple juice
freshly squeezed orange juice	orange juice
milk	soy milk
coffee beans	brewed coffee
tap water	mineral water
potatoes	sweet potatoes
tampons	nappies, diapers (US)
glasses	hearing aids
salt	road salt
flowers + leaves (if fresh)	flowers + leaves (if dried)
local public transport	regional public transport
wheelchairs	stair lifts
fertilizer	potting soil
McDonald's (take-away)	McDonald's (eat-in)

On the other hand, doctors, dentists, physiotherapists, midwives, hospitals, theatres, museums, zoos, orchestras, schools, universities, house rent, bank loans and stamps do not attract any VAT.

1. Are the differences justified in your opinion?
2. Do you know other examples that you find hard to explain?
3. Are there any specific items you would tax differently, or not at all?

> VAT rates can be changed to temporarily relieve consumers and boost the economy. This was done during the COVID pandemic.

4 Corporate taxation

 Discuss the following questions.

1 How are companies taxed? Does it depend on their type or size?
2 Are companies themselves taxed, or their owners?
3 What is important when advising on start-up matters?
4 What questions would you ask?
5 Can you give examples of businesses (e.g. hairdressers, restaurants, car sellers) that typically favour a specific legal structure?

🔊 07 **1** Alexander and Tim Dudziak from Poland want to set up a business in Germany. They have arranged for a consultation with Anna Springer, a professional German tax advisor.

a **Listen to their conversation and answer the questions.**

1 What sort of start-up are they planning?
2 Do they talk about specific taxes?
3 Does Anna mention any legal structures?
4 What do 6%, 8-9%, 15%, and € 24,500 refer to?

b **Listen again and complete the sentences.**

1 From what I've read on the internet there are several _____ of businesses we could opt for.

2 In partnerships, every partner is taxed individually, whereas corporations are taxed as an _____.

3 Then there is trade tax, _____ on profits of trading businesses.

4 So VAT is an ongoing issue, whereas trade and corporation tax are _____ yearly.

5 When you compare the taxation of partnerships and corporations, I can tell you that the difference isn't _____ and may add up to around 6%.

6 _____ might be an issue.

7 Or the _____ volume.

> **VOCABULARY**
>
> to **assess sth**
>   etw. festsetzen
> **corporation tax**
>   Körperschaftsteuer
> **entity** Körperschaft,
>   juristische Person
> **liability** Haftung
> **trade tax** Gewerbesteuer

ENGLISH FOR TAX PROFESSIONALS

c **Discuss the following questions.**

1 Does it make sense to choose the structure of your business on the basis of taxation?
2 Are there other aspects you would always address when advising start-ups?
3 When you advise somebody who wants to run a business on their own, are there more, fewer or other options compared to partnering up with others?

> **DID YOU KNOW?**
>
> **Business types** that exist in one country do not necessarily have an equivalent in another one. It can therefore be difficult to provide a proper translation. In most countries, there are different kinds of partnerships and limited companies. A type that is widespread in Germany, the *GmbH & Co. KG*, is unknown in both Britain and the US. Such entities must be described in a way that gives the listener an idea of what you are referring to. The entity mentioned could be described as a limited partnership that has a limited company as a general partner.
> Another example is the *Unternehmergesellschaft*, also referred to as a *Mini-GmbH*. Here, the share capital is important as only €1 is required to set up such a company.
>
> | Germany | UK | US |
> |---|---|---|
> | Personengesellschaft | partnership | partnership |
> | Kapitalgesellschaft | limited company | corporation |
> | Einzelunternehmen | sole proprietorship | sole proprietorship |
> | GbR | civil law partnership | partnership constituted under civil law |
> | OHG | ordinary partnership | general partnership |
> | KG | limited partnership | limited partnership |
> | GmbH | private limited company | privately held corporation |
> | AG | public limited company | publicly traded corporation |
>
> If you want to distinguish a *Personengesellschaft* from a *Partnerschaftsgesellschaft*, you can refer to the latter as a "professional partnership".

2 Anna promised to provide further information on the issues discussed.

 a **Explain the legal structures mentioned in the table. Then draft the table in English.**

	Einzel-unternehmen	GbR	OHG	KG	GmbH & Co. KG	UG	GmbH	AG
Mindest-kapital	nein	nein	nein	nein	ja	ja	ja	ja
Haftung	voll	voll	voll	beschränkt	beschränkt	beschränkt	beschränkt	beschränkt
Forma-litäten	gering	gering	hoch	hoch	hoch	gering*	gering*	hoch

*mit Musterprotokoll

b **Prepare a client questionnaire to collect information on client expectations regarding the three items in the left column of the table above. Would you include other issues?**

 c **Discuss the pros & cons of these legal structures. Which one(s) would you recommend in Alexander's and Tim's case?**

3 A few weeks after their meeting, Anna Springer is having a video call with Alexander Dudziak. Read their dialogue and answer the questions.

Anna: I know it was a lot, but did you have a chance to look at the materials I sent you?
Alexander: Yes, I did, but I'm still confused about trade tax. Is every business affected?
Anna: Every business run in Germany is subject to trade tax. Self-employed professionals, farming, forestry and non-profit organisations are not affected. Traditionally commercial businesses have been liable to trade tax in Germany no matter what legal form they have. Sole proprietorships and partnerships are subject to trade tax just the same as companies. And limited companies are liable regardless of the industry they are involved in.
Alexander: Complicated. So companies pay a national and a local tax.
Anna: That's right. Trade tax is a local tax which is levied on an annual basis with about 15%, but there are major differences depending on where the business is located. Every municipality has its own factor.
Alexander: And how is this tax assessed?
Anna: The tax office calculates the trade earnings from the company's profit by considering specific add-backs, deductions and tax-free amounts. Then it applies a basic trade tax rate of 3.5% and notifies the local municipality about the trade tax assessment base it has determined. The municipality then works out the actual trade tax. It does so by applying the local percentage rate. This percentage rate is the municipal trade tax factor.
Alexander: I see. I've always envied you for your low corporate taxes, but I have to change my mind. We are far better off with our 19% and no local taxes in Poland.

1 Does every business pay tax, independent of its legal form?
2 What kind of tax is trade tax, and who collects it?
3 What is the basic tax rate?

4 Match the following items with their English equivalents.

1 Hinzurechnungen
2 Abzüge
3 Gewerbeertrag
4 Gewerbesteuermessbetrag
5 Gewerbesteuermesszahl
6 Gewerbesteuerhebesatz
7 Steuerfreibetrag
8 Landwirtschaft
9 Forstwirtschaft
10 Gemeinnützige Einrichtung

a tax-free amount
b trade tax factor
c farming
d deductions
e trade earnings
f non-profit organization
g add-backs
h trade tax assessment base
i basic trade tax rate
j forestry

> **DID YOU KNOW?**
>
> The tax base for **corporate income tax (CIT)** is not necessarily the balance sheet. **Add-backs** and **deductions** play an important role. **Hidden profit distributions**, also known as **constructive dividends**, can have an impact. Certain benefits must pass an **arm's length test** (*Fremdvergleich*) to be accepted by the tax authorities.

5 Complete the formula on the right for the calculation of trade tax. Use the information from the previous two exercises.

company's profit
+ _____
− _____
(if applicable) − _____
= _____
x 3.5 % _____
= _____
x _____
= trade tax

ENGLISH FOR TAX PROFESSIONALS

6 Addressing can be difficult. Read the Useful Phrases and the tips. Can you add any other?

> **USEFUL PHRASES** Email writing
>
> **Salutations**
> - Dear Sir or Madam
> - Dear Madam/Sir
> - To whom it may concern
> - Dear Ms Hudson
> - Dear Mr Hernandez
> - Dear Jennifer
> - Dear project team
> - Dear all
> - Hi Tim
> - Annie
>
> **Closings**
> - Yours faithfully (BE) (*only in formal writing + when recipient's name unknown*)
> - Yours sincerely/truly/cordially (BE)
> - Sincerely/Truly/Cordially (yours) (AE)
> - Kind/Best regards
> - Best wishes

*In **American English** a full stop is usually placed after the title (Ms./Mr.), and a comma after both salutation and closing. A colon can be used instead of a comma after the salutation. In **British English** none of this is needed.*

*Despite the differences in global English, one rule is to always **capitalize** the first word after the salutation. It is also advisable to write out the month in full to avoid confusion about the **date format** which begins with the day in BE, but with the month in AE.*

Which of the following expressions should be improved? Give reasons for your decision.

1 13.03.2028
To whom it may concern
Best Regards

2 1. March 2032
Dear team
Kind Regards

3 01/03/25
Dear Madams and Sirs
Yours very truly

4 1st March 2030
Dear Professor Dr Durand
With Kind regards

*If a person has more than one **title**, use only one in English.*

*(Dear Dr Hernandez
NOT: ~~Dear Ms Dr Hernandez~~)*

7 Read the following email. Calculate the tax mentioned, assuming an ordinary partnership operation (no add-backs or deductions, Berlin's trade tax faxtor is 410%). Then, do some research on tax factors of municipalities near Berlin. Draft a reply.

Dear Ms Springer
With reference to our above-mentioned business, we would like to approach you with some queries regarding our tax filings.
First of all, we would like to ask you to advise us on our trade tax burden. Our bookkeeping department has already calculated our taxable income for last year. It amounts to € 100,000.
Secondly, we would like to know whether we could save taxes by simply moving our office outside Berlin. Please do the necessary research and provide us with suitable information.
We look forward to hearing from you.

Yours sincerely
Alexander Dudziak

> **DID YOU KNOW?**
>
> **Accounting** follows certain **standards**. Many countries have established generally accepted accounting principles (GAAP). Freelancers and smaller businesses often apply a **cash accounting** (*Überschussrechnung*) method, whereas larger companies operate on an **accrual basis** (*periodengerechte Abgrenzung*). The internationally most widely accepted standards are the International Financial Reporting Standards (IFRS), which are mandated or accepted by more than 130 countries. National GAAP still differ, but a set of certain **financial statements** (*Jahresabschluss*), such as a **balance sheet** and a **profit & loss (P&L) account/statement**, and certain **items** (*Posten*), such as assets, liabilities and equity, are required everywhere.

UNIT 4: CORPORATE TAXATION

8 Discuss the following questions.

1. How many statements are required under German GAAP? Can you name them?
2. How does this compare to IFRS?
3. Are you aware of any differences between German GAAP and IFRS?
4. Are companies required or allowed to use IFRS in your country?

9 Categorise the following terms into IFRS and German GAAP. Add "I" (IFRS) or "G" (German GAAP) to the boxes.

1. balance sheet
2. notes
3. profit & loss account
4. statement of cash flows
5. statement of changes in equity
6. statement of financial position
7. statement of profit and loss and other comprehensive income

10 What are the different statements about? Fill the gaps with key terms from the box.

expenses | owners' | current (2x) | intangible | retained | non-current (2x) | reporting | assets | liabilities | activities

> **VOCABULARY**
>
> **assets** Aktiva, Vermögenswerte
> **current assets** Umlaufvermögen
> **current liabilities** kurzfristige Verbindlichkeiten
> **liabilities (pl.)** Passiva, Verbindlichkeiten
> **non-current assets** Anlagevermögen
> **non-current liabilities** langfristige Verbindlichkeiten
> to **retain sth** etw. ein-/zurückbehalten
> **retained earnings (pl.)** Gewinnvortrag

A **balance sheet** is divided into two parts that "balance each other out".

Formula: _____¹ = _____² + shareholders' equity

Assets are what a company uses to operate its business. Shareholders' or _____³ equity, is the amount of money invested, plus any re-invested or _____⁴ earnings over time. On the balance sheet, assets appear on the top or left, liabilities and shareholders' equity appear below or to the right. Short-term or _____⁵ assets remain with a company for up to a year. Examples include cash and goods for sale. Long-term or _____⁶ assets remain with the company for a longer period of time. Examples include machinery and buildings, or _____⁷ assets, such as patents and trademarks. Liabilities have the same distinction: they must be settled either within one year (_____⁸) or later (_____⁹).

An **income statement** reflects the profit or loss made.

Formula: revenue – _____¹⁰ = profit/loss

A **cash flow statement** summarizes the amount of cash going in and out of a company, broken down into operating, investing and financing _____¹¹. A **statement of changes in equity** shows the share capital at the beginning and the end of the _____¹² period, considering profits made, dividends paid and any other changes. The **notes** comprise a summary of accounting policies and other explanatory information.

ENGLISH FOR TAX PROFESSIONALS

11 Match these official IFRS terms by adding the letters a-n to the boxes.

1 statement of financial position
2 statement of profit and loss and other comprehensive income
3 statement of cash flows
4 statement of changes in equity
5 notes
6 property, plant and equipment
7 intangible assets
8 inventories
9 trade and other receivables
10 cash and cash equivalents
11 trade and other payables
12 provisions
13 current tax liabilities and current tax assets
14 deferred tax liabilities and deferred tax assets

a Vorräte
b Zahlungsmittel und Zahlungsmitteläquivalente
c latente Steueransprüche und -schulden
d Eigenkapitalveränderungsrechnung
e Verbindlichkeiten aus Lieferungen und Leistungen und sonstige Verbindlichkeiten
f Steuerschulden und -ansprüche
g Bilanz
h Rückstellungen
i Kapitalflussrechnung
j immaterielle Vermögenswerte
k Forderungen aus Lieferungen und Leistungen und sonstige Forderungen
l Gesamtergebnisrechnung
m Sachanlagen
n Anhang

1	2	3	4	5	6	7	8	9	10	11	12	13	14

12 Put the following expressions into the table. Then, analyse the financial statements in the appendix and use the expressions to describe the developments regarding the company's assets, liabilities, equity and profit over the reporting periods.

▷ p. 56

to decrease | to fluctuate | to hit a low | to increase | to reach a peak | to remain steady | to take off | to slump

Upward movement	Downward movement	Other

13 SIMULATION

Hold a meeting to discuss reporting requirements of companies you are dealing with.
Make some notes on the types of businesses you advise, as well as accounting methods available to them. Then compare and discuss with other members of the group.

	Cash or balance sheet accounting, German GAAP or IFRS?
Sole traders	
Partnerships	
Limited companies	

14 MEDIATION

A topic many people are worried about is *Scheinselbständigkeit*. Use the information to draft a summary for your clients. Explain the differences between employees and freelancers, describe the criteria for assessing their status, and outline the risks for your clients as potential employers.

Arbeitnehmer	Selbständiger
abhängig	unabhängig
weisungsgebunden	weisungsfrei
festgelegte Arbeitszeiten	freie Zeiteinteilung
bezahlter Urlaub	kein Urlaub
Lohnfortzahlung im Krankheitsfall	keine Zahlung im Krankheitsfall

> **VOCABULARY**
>
> **bogus self-employment** Scheinselbständigkeit
> **instructions** Weisungen
> **sick pay** Lohnfortzahlung

§ 611a BGB: Durch den Arbeitsvertrag wird der Arbeitnehmer im Dienste eines anderen zur Leistung weisungsgebundener, fremdbestimmter Arbeit in persönlicher Abhängigkeit verpflichtet. Das Weisungsrecht kann Inhalt, Durchführung, Zeit und Ort der Tätigkeit betreffen. Weisungsgebunden ist, wer nicht im Wesentlichen frei seine Tätigkeit gestalten und seine Arbeitszeit bestimmen kann. Der Grad der persönlichen Abhängigkeit hängt dabei auch von der Eigenart der jeweiligen Tätigkeit ab. Für die Feststellung, ob ein Arbeitsvertrag vorliegt, ist eine Gesamtbetrachtung aller Umstände vorzunehmen. Zeigt die tatsächliche Durchführung des Vertragsverhältnisses, dass es sich um ein Arbeitsverhältnis handelt, kommt es auf die Bezeichnung im Vertrag nicht an.

15 Can you complete the words?

1. pr_v_____n → you make this for future payments
2. _ed_ct_on → this reduces your tax burden
3. _dd-_a_k → this is something you have to consider when calculating trade tax
4. l__b_l_t_ → payables
5. __ss__ss → the process of determining taxes to be paid
6. l_v_ → to charge something, e.g. fees or taxes
7. _r_d → one type of corporate income
8. c_rp_r_t_ → another word for company
9. _nt_t_ → yet another word for company
10. __ss_t → something that is yours

> *There are many ways to refer to a **business**: company/enterprise/firm/undertaking* – *and a few more. **Firms** are usually partnerships. **Undertaking** is a rather uncommon and ambiguous term as it can also be a job or task, or a promise to do something.*

ENGLISH FOR TAX PROFESSIONALS

OVER TO YOU

Corporate taxation in the UK, US and Europe

UK companies are taxed at 25%. A small profits rate (SPR) of 19% applies to profits not exceeding £50,000. Profits between £50,001 and £250,000 are taxed at a rate of 26.5%. This is called "marginal relief". If a company makes at least £250,000, the complete amount is taxed at 25%. Certain sectors are subject to special regimes that attract higher or lower taxes. These include, among others, oil and gas, life insurance, banking and real estate investment trusts (REIT). There is no additional local tax regime, such as a municipal trade tax, in the UK.

The US have both federal and state corporate income taxes. The federal rate is 21%. Further taxes of up to 11.5% may apply, depending on where the company is based. North Carolina is at the bottom (2.5%), New Jersey at the top end. No taxes are levied by Nevada, South Dakota and Wyoming. The average combined federal and state corporate income tax rate is 25.89%.

In Europe, Hungary and Ireland have the lowest, Portugal and Malta the highest rates. Guernsey and Jersey do not tax corporations at all. The OECD is working towards a global minimum tax rate of 15%, on which the EU passed a directive. This means that companies with an annual turnover of at least €750m pay the minimum rate no matter where they make their money. This a move towards fair taxation and combatting tax avoidance.

> **DID YOU KNOW?**
>
> The **Organisation for Economic Co-operation and Development (OECD)** is an international organisation establishing standards and finding solutions to a range of social, economic and environmental challenges. It plays a key role in achieving **fair taxation**, **enhancing transparency** and **promoting the exchange of financial information**. It also provides comprehensive data on corporate taxes around the world. The EU, alongside more than 140 countries, follows the OECD's **minimum taxation model**, ensuring that companies pay at least 15% on their income. This goes together with rules on how to better deal with activities designed to shift profits to low- or no-tax countries. Subsidiaries established in such countries are often used to handle investments, products, loans, interest and dividend payments in a way that they are not taxed appropriately. With these rules in place, governments expect to cash in $220bn in additional taxes every year.

1. How do these figures compare to your country?

2. Do you know how corporate taxation has developed over the last decades?

3. Are there any tax havens in your country that attract companies by offering low taxes?

IN THIS UNIT YOU WILL …
- look at VAT in the EU
- deal with double taxation agreements
- discuss tax avoidance

5 International taxation

 Discuss the following questions.

1. What do you know about VAT rates and rules in the EU?
2. How does EU legislation affect international trade?
3. Can you explain the concept of triangulation?

1 Chen Garments is a Chinese textile company with operations in Europe, Africa and South America.

🔊 **a** Listen to a conference call chaired by Chen Garments' CFO, Huan Ling, and complete the diagram
08   by adding the words from the box to the arrows.

invoicing (2x) | order | sourcing | supply

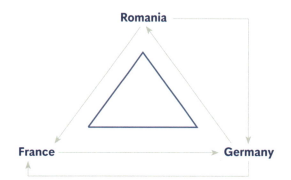

VOCABULARY

(intra-Community) acquisition
  (innergemeinschaftlicher) Erwerb
(intra-Community) supply
  (innergemeinschaftliche) Lieferung
red tape Verwaltungsaufwand, Bürokratie

to **source sth** etw. beziehen
subsidiary Tochtergesellschaft
triangulation Dreiecksgeschäft
to **zero-rate sth** etw. umsatzsteuerfrei
  behandeln

38 | ENGLISH FOR TAX PROFESSIONALS

b Add the terms to the correct definition.

frontiers | intra-Community acquisition | intra-Community supply | triangulation | zero-rate

1 sale within the EU: _____
2 purchase within the EU: _____
3 charging VAT at a rate of 0%: _____
4 physical borders or boundaries between countries: _____
5 simplification of EU trade involving three parties: _____

c Listen again and choose the correct answer.

1 What is the primary purpose of the meeting?
   ▢ Discussing new business opportunities
   ▢ VAT accounting in dealings with the EU
   ▢ Introducing a new supplier from Romania
   ▢ Exploring marketing strategies

2 What role does the German company play in the proposed VAT triangulation process?
   ▢ It directly supplies goods to the French customer.
   ▢ It acts as an intermediary between the Romanian supplier and the French customer.
   ▢ It registers for VAT in every member state involved.
   ▢ It is not involved in the supply.

3 What is Luise Ganter's response when asked about handling orders in EU countries where the Argentinian company is not registered for VAT?
   ▢ The Romanian company will make a VAT-inclusive supply.
   ▢ The Argentinian company will make a VAT-inclusive supply.
   ▢ The German company will handle the orders to simplify the process.
   ▢ Triangulation rules cannot be applied in this case.

4 According to Luise Ganter, when can a company take advantage of the VAT triangulation regime?
   ▢ Only if it is registered for VAT in every EU member state.
   ▢ As long as the three companies involved are all in the EU.
   ▢ Only when more than three companies are involved in the transaction.
   ▢ When the goods physically cross the frontiers of the countries involved.

d Are the following statements true or false?   True   False

1 Triangulation can be applied regardless of the number of companies involved in the transaction.
2 Triangulation is a mechanism in EU trade involving three parties physically passing goods from one to the next.
3 If the Romanian company supplied directly to the French customer without involving the German company, the German company would have VAT obligations in France.
4 If the Argentinian company was registered for VAT in France, the Romanian trader could zero-rate the goods for VAT.
5 The German business suggests handling all trade within the European Union to save time and money.

e Explain the term "red tape" as it is used in the context of Huan's remark on minimising it in their dealings with EU countries. What exactly helps reducing it?

UNIT 5: INTERNATIONAL TAXATION

2 There are special rules on VAT in EU trade. Read the text and complete the exercises below.

Each EU country has a **standard rate** of at least **15%**. One or two **reduced rates** of at least **5%** may apply to specific goods and services. VAT is based on the **country-of-destination principle**. This means taxes are levied in the country where the goods or services are consumed, ensuring that businesses pay VAT in the country where they make their sales. In B2B transactions, the supplier does not charge VAT, and the buyer is responsible for accounting for the VAT through a mechanism known as **reverse charge**.

Specific rules apply to B2C transactions. Because of the destination principle, suppliers would normally have to register for VAT in every country they supply to. However, a scheme known as **one stop shop (OSS)** allows you to declare and pay VAT in your own country, accounting for the VAT due in others. This applies to **distance sales** of goods and services. You can still apply your own VAT rate if the total value of your distance sales and **telecommunications, broadcasting and electronic (TBE) services** do not exceed €10,000. In this case, the country-of-destination principle shifts to the **country-of-origin principle**, which means your supply is deemed a domestic one. OSS is not relevant in this situation as you account for VAT in your domestic return. There are a few notable exceptions:
- A house is taxed where it is located. For example, if an architect based in France is hired to design a house in Spain, the architect's fee will be subject to Spanish VAT.
- Passenger transport is taxed according to the distance covered. For example, if the price of a bus ticket for a journey from Poland to France via Germany will include Polish, German and French VAT, in proportion to the distance covered in each country. If the bus also travels via Switzerland, there will be no EU VAT on that part of the journey, as Switzerland is not an EU country.
- Restaurants and catering (other than those on ships, aircraft or trains) are taxed at the place where the services are physically carried out. For example, if a company based in Luxembourg supplies food and drinks for an event in Florence, the company must charge Italian VAT.
- If you buy a new car (or a motorbike or boat) in another EU country, VAT is paid in the country where you import and register it, i.e. your country of residence.

VOCABULARY

country-of-destination principle
  Bestimmungslandprinzip
country-of-origin principle
  Ursprungslandprinzip
to **deem sth** etw. ansehen/betrachten
distance sales Fernverkäufe
domestic inländisch
reverse charge Umkehrung der
  Steuerschuldnerschaft

a Explain the expressions "distance sales" and "electronic services".

b Discuss the reverse charge mechanism. How does it work? Why is it in place? What are its advantages?

  c Discuss the following scenarios with a partner.

1 Mareijke from the Netherlands orders a book from a large online retailer in Ireland. The price of the book is €10. What price will appear when she enters her address and clicks "pay"?
2 Mette lives in Sweden and often purchases eBooks from a major Finnish online book seller. Will the Finnish supplier charge Swedish or Finnish VAT?
3 Joao runs a consultancy company which is based in Lisbon. He provides consulting services to a private individual living in Copenhagen. Will he charge Danish or Portuguese VAT?
4 A German craftsman not making more than €10,000 abroad repairs a machine in Austria. Can he charge German VAT?
5 Gina from Berlin teaches English online to a student in Budapest. What VAT rate applies? Can she use the OSS system?

ENGLISH FOR TAX PROFESSIONALS

3 SIMULATION

Prepare a meeting to discuss VAT in the EU. Draft a table with different scenarios regarding B2B and B2C transactions originating in your country, covering different goods and services, the applicable VAT rates, reverse charge and simplification mechanisms that may apply. Choose any goods and services, and an EU country of supply. Then, select one person to chair the meeting and discuss the scenarios, taking turns with other members in your group. Use the Useful Phrases to help you.

	Goods/Services	Country of supply	VAT rate of (country)	Reverse charge/ OSS/other
Goods (B2B)				
Services (B2B)				
Goods (B2C)				
Services (B2C)				

USEFUL PHRASES   Holding meetings, tele- and videoconferences

Opening, chairing and closing
- Good morning, everybody.
- Can we start?
- Let's get down to business.
- Who's going to take the minutes?
- The purpose of our conference is …
- Our aim today is …
- There are three items on the agenda.
- Ali, would you like to start?
- Anything to add, Agniezska?
- Let's move on to the next item.
- Let me summarize the main points.
- Is there any other business?
- OK, thank you for all your contributions.

Taking part
- In my opinion …
- To my mind …
- In my view …
- I think / believe / suppose / assume / guess …
- I agree with you.
- I'm with Fatma on this.
- I'm afraid I can't agree with that.
- I see it rather differently.
- Can I just say at this point that …
- May I just come back to a point that Jim made?
- I didn't quite catch that.
- Do you see what I mean?
- Let me put it another way.

The **chairperson** kicks off the meeting or conference (welcome and purpose) and structures the discussion by acting as facilitator, asking for opinions and summarizing **action items**. There might be an **agenda** to follow and **minutes** to take.

UNIT 5: INTERNATIONAL TAXATION

4 Discuss the following questions on key concepts of international taxation.

1 In what countries are individuals and businesses taxed?
2 What rules apply to the digital economy?
3 How do double taxation agreements help?

5 Listen to a talk on various aspects of international taxation.

a Mark the answers to the questions.

1 What does the 183-day rule determine?
- Eligibility for tax credits
- Residency and tax liability
- Types of foreign income
- Legal methods to minimize taxes

2 Why is transfer pricing mentioned in the text?
- To discuss legal methods of minimizing taxes
- To explain the concept of permanent establishment
- To prevent profit shifting and tax avoidance in related entity transactions
- To highlight the importance of tax credits

3 What is base erosion and profit shifting (BEPS)?
- Legal methods to minimize taxes
- Exploiting gaps and mismatches in tax rules to shift profits artificially
- A type of tax evasion
- The concept of permanent establishment

> **VOCABULARY**
> **base erosion and profit shifting** Gewinnverkürzung und Gewinnverlagerung
> **credit** *hier:* Anrechnung
> **entity** *hier:* Unternehmen
> **exemption** *hier:* Freistellung
> **group company** Konzerngesellschaft
> **permanent establishment** Betriebsstätte
> **residence** Wohnsitz
> **tax avoidance** Steuervermeidung
> **tax evasion** Steuerhinterziehung
> **transfer pricing** Verrechnungspreise

b Add the missing words.

1 The two main principles of international taxation: _____ , _____
2 The amount of days you need to spend in most countries to be considered a resident: _____
3 A fixed place of business giving rise to tax liability: _____
4 Two methods to account for taxes paid elsewhere: _____ , _____
5 Reducing your tax burden by legal or illegal means: _____ , _____
6 Rules for transactions with subsidiaries: _____
7 A place you go to in order to save taxes: _____
8 Moving company profits to low-tax countries: _____ , _____

c Explain the concept of permanent establishment. Provide examples.

d In what ways might tax avoidance, though legal, be controversial? Give examples of how taxes are avoided. Can you name companies and countries often mentioned in this context?

ENGLISH FOR TAX PROFESSIONALS

6 MEDIATION

You have received the enquiry on the right from a Canadian company.
Draft an email reply explaining the provisions of the German-Canadian double taxation agreement relevant in this case.

> We produce kitchenware and own a warehouse near Berlin from where we deliver to customers in Europe. In the next years, we plan to build a factory next to it, which we want to use for producing spare parts. We also plan to lease parts of our warehouse building as we are not using its entire space.
> Could you tell us where our profits will be taxed now and in the future? We would like to know whether we have to pay taxes in Germany, and if so, to what extent.
>
> Thank you for your assistance.

Abkommen zwischen der Bundesrepublik Deutschland und Kanada zur Vermeidung der Doppelbesteuerung

Artikel 5
Im Sinne dieses Abkommens bedeutet der Ausdruck „Betriebsstätte" eine feste Geschäftseinrichtung, durch die die Tätigkeit eines Unternehmens ganz oder teilweise ausgeübt wird. Er umfasst insbesondere:

a) einen Ort der Leitung;
b) eine Zweigniederlassung;
c) eine Geschäftsstelle;
d) eine Fabrikationsstätte;
e) eine Werkstätte.

Ungeachtet der vorstehenden Bestimmungen dieses Artikels gelten nicht als Betriebsstätten Einrichtungen, die ausschließlich zur Lagerung, Ausstellung oder Auslieferung von Gütern oder Waren des Unternehmens benutzt werden.

Artikel 6
Einkünfte, die eine in einem Vertragsstaat ansässige Person aus unbeweglichem Vermögen bezieht, das im anderen Vertragsstaat liegt, können im anderen Staat besteuert werden.

Artikel 7
Gewinne eines Unternehmens eines Vertragsstaats können nur in diesem Staat besteuert werden, es sei denn, dass das Unternehmen seine Tätigkeit im anderen Vertragsstaat durch eine dort gelegene Betriebsstätte ausübt oder ausgeübt hat. Übt das Unternehmen seine Tätigkeit auf diese Weise aus oder hat es sie so ausgeübt, so können die Gewinne des Unternehmens im anderen Staat besteuert werden, jedoch nur insoweit, als sie dieser Betriebsstätte zugerechnet werden können.

(BGBl. 2002 II 11, S. 671 ff.)

> Agreements between states are also referred to as **conventions** or **treaties**. They are sometimes amended by a **protocol**.

 7 Discuss in class what measures could be taken to achieve fair taxation, discourage profit shifting and promote international cooperation.

8 Read the following text and explain the three criteria mentioned in your own words to a partner.

> Many governments and organisations have been fighting tax avoidance for ages. The EU maintains a list of non-cooperative countries, based on a number of criteria relating to **transparency**, **fair taxation** and **anti-BEPS measures**. The IMF lists offshore financial centres, the OECD countries in which citizenship can easily be acquired by investing money, thus giving access to taxation models and rights only citizens have.
>
> **Transparency** allows states to have access to data on the foreign assets of their citizens so that they cannot hide and escape taxation. Countries should regularly and automatically exchange data. The OECD has developed a common reporting standard (CRS), on which many countries rely, and a standard on the exchange of information on request. It also drafted a convention on mutual administrative assistance in tax matters.
>
> **Fair taxation** addresses harmful tax practices, whereby financial flows are attracted that do not reflect real economic activity. This includes offshore structures with no or very low corporate income tax, which should go along with a minimum number of employees, facilities and other real economic ties.
>
> **Anti-BEPS measures** involve complying with minimum standards on harmful tax measures, treaty shopping, country-by-country reporting and dispute resolution.

Use the internet to find out how many countries are currently "blacklisted" by the OECD, the IMF and the EU. Are there any countries you would (not) have expected?

> **DID YOU KNOW?**
> It can be quite tricky to talk about corporate structures, especially when you have German terminology in mind (*Muttergesellschaft*, *Tochtergesellschaft*, *Konzern*, *verbundenes Unternehmen*). Do not fall for false friends: there are no "mothers" or "daughters", and they are certainly not "connected" in a "concern". The correct terms are **parent company**, **subsidiary** and **group**. They are **affiliated** or **associated (companies)**, or simply **affiliates** or **associates**. A company's type of **interest**, **share** or **stake** determines whether we refer to **affiliated/associated companies** or **subsidiaries**. You can use the terms **affiliate** and **associate** in the same way to refer to a company whose parent is a **minority shareholder**, or has a **minority interest**, of less than 50%. A **subsidiary** is a company whose parent is a **majority shareholder**, or has a **majority interest**, of more than 50%. When a parent company owns 100% of the subsidiary, we speak of a **wholly-owned subsidiary**.

9 The world of accounting is full of acronyms. Do you know what they stand for? Look through the unit for help.

1
2
3
4
5
6
7
8
9
10

 With a partner, discuss other acronyms in the context of accounting and explain them in class. Look at page 80 for more examples.

ENGLISH FOR TAX PROFESSIONALS

OVER TO YOU

Too clever to be taxed?

Some multinational companies are infamous for shifting their profits on a large scale. They make billions, but pay fairly little in taxes. This is done by registering in low-tax countries, but doing substantial business elsewhere. You can, for instance, make a lot of money with a mobile app without having an office or employees in a particular country. Still, users in that country making in-app purchases or watching online ads can mean a lot of income. Accounting for earnings at a destination of your choice is often possible, but more and more countries are taking measures to make it more difficult to escape taxation. As tax systems often rely on the concept of a permanent establishment that involves a physical presence, the digital economy and its taxation pose a particular challenge. Countries around the world, as well as international organizations, are harmonising rules to deal with this issue.

One reaction has been the introduction of a "Google tax". It has become a synonym for the taxation of diverted profits. Famous for establishing itself in a low tax capital (Dublin), Google managed to keep its tax bill low. They did so by selling licences to use its search engine to a subsidiary on the Bermudas (a tax haven), which then sold them to their Irish subsidiary. These payments would normally be subject to taxation, but a company in the Netherlands was placed in between them. Thus, the licences were granted by a company in Europe, exempting them from taxation under the EU Interest and Royalty Directive, which provides for non-taxation of such income between member states. Other large multinationals, including technology giants, used similar methods, involving foreign companies, dividends, royalties, loans, interest, and the transfer of intellectual property (IP). For example, a company based in country A (a tax haven) grants a loan to a subsidiary in country B, which makes high interest payments in return. These payments are then deductible in country B and not taxable in country A.

The EU introduced legislation mandating a minimum corporate tax rate of 15% no matter where companies are registered. The UK and Australia passed similar laws, imposing rates of 25% and 40%, respectively. The US Securities and Exchange Commission (SEC) makes businesses publish details on where and how they derive their worldwide income. Authorities of other countries can use this data to identify and tackle tax avoidance measures taken by these businesses.

1 Are you aware of any existing legislation, measures or plans combatting such methods in your country, or the EU?
2 Do you consider these measures to be sufficient? Would you look at other aspects?
3 Check the OECD website for their actions against profit shifting and discuss whether the items they mention adequately address the challenge.

VOCABULARY

to **derive sth** *hier:* etw. erzielen
to **divert sth** etw. umleiten
intellectual property geistiges Eigentum
loan Kredit, Darlehn
to **mandate sth** etw. vorschreiben
to **pose a challenge** eine Herausforderung darstellen
royalty Lizenzgebühr

UNIT 5: INTERNATIONAL TAXATION

IN THIS UNIT YOU WILL ...

- explore various types of auditing
- discuss the roles of auditors in the corporate world
- address accounting fraud and liability

6 Working in auditing

What do you know about auditing? Discuss the following questions.

1 How would you define auditing?
2 What is the difference between internal and external auditing?
3 Are there any other types of auditing?

 1 Read the text. Then, on the next page, mark the statements that are true. Give reasons for your answer.

Auditing is the systematic examination and evaluation of financial information, records, statements, or any other relevant data. The purpose of auditing is to provide an independent and objective assessment of the accuracy, completeness, and reliability of information. Auditing is commonly associated with **financial audits**, where auditors review financial statements to ensure they present a **true and fair view** of an organization's financial position and performance. Here are some types of auditing:

- **Financial Auditing**:
  - **External Audit**: Conducted by external auditors who are independent of the organization. It ensures that financial statements are free from material misstatements.
  - **Internal Audit**: Conducted by internal auditors who are employees of the organization. It focuses on internal controls, risk management, and operational efficiency.
- **Compliance Auditing**: Ensures that an organization is adhering to relevant laws, regulations, and internal policies.
- **Information Systems (IS) Auditing**: Evaluates the controls and security measures of information systems to ensure the confidentiality, integrity, and availability of data.
- **Environmental Auditing**: Reviews an organization's adherence to environmental regulations and sustainability practices.
- **Forensic Auditing**: Conducted to investigate cases of misconduct, including fraud.

VOCABULARY

accountability Rechenschaft, Verantwortung
to **adhere to sth** etw. befolgen, einhalten
assessment Beurteilung
confidentiality Geheimhaltung, Vertraulichkeit
misstatement Falschdarstellung
policy Richtlinie
sampling Stichproben
stakeholder Akteur*in, Interessenvertreter*in
sustainability Nachhaltigkeit
true and fair view ein den tatsächlichen Verhältnissen entsprechendes Bild

ENGLISH FOR TAX PROFESSIONALS

Auditing plays a crucial role in ensuring transparency, accountability, and trust in financial and operational reporting. Auditors use various techniques, including sampling, interviews, and document reviews, to gather evidence and draw conclusions about the reliability of the information being audited. The ultimate goal is to provide stakeholders with assurance regarding the accuracy and integrity of the information under review.

1 In financial auditing, external and internal auditors can be distinguished in the following ways:

External auditors …
- are staff members of the companies they audit.
- are independent.
- assess the performance of companies and their management.

Internal auditors …
- only work for one company.
- officially confirm the accuracy of financial statements.
- are independent.

2 The overall aim of financial auditing is to assure that financial statements …
- include all data available.
- fairly present a company's financial standing.
- do not include errors.

3 Forensic Auditing/Accounting is conducted when …
- a merger is about to happen.
- a crime might have occurred.
- dividends are paid.

4 Material misstatements …
- involve minor errors.
- are mistakes of a significant nature.
- potentially draw a false picture of a company's standing.

5 Auditing is done for …
- directors only.
- investors only.
- stakeholders.

2 Listen to a conversation between an external and an internal auditor and write down the four specific control areas they discuss.

1 _____
2 _____
3 _____
4 _____

Now answer the following questions.

1 What type of transactions does the internal auditor identify in the context of their approval workflows?
2 What focus is the external auditor happy about after his question on IT has been answered?
3 What type of program is in place with the company to deal with irregularities?

VOCABULARY

to **align sth** etw. in Einklang bringen
to **enhance sth** etw. verbessern
layer *hier:* Ebene
thorough gründlich
vulnerability *hier:* Schwäche
to **walk sb through sth** mit jmdm. etw. durchgehen

A **penetration test** (also known as a **pentest** or **ethical hacking**) is a **simulated cyberattack** on a computer system. It is performed to identify weaknesses that might allow hackers to infiltrate it, steal data and cause harm.

UNIT 6: WORKING IN AUDITING

3 Read the text on accounting scandals. Then match the words from the text with their German equivalents.

With many accounting scandals in mind, detecting and investigating fraud is important to preserve a company's standing and reputation. White collar crimes, such as bribery, embezzlement and money laundering, are often involved. There are many areas of concern, including business valuation, taxes, securities, bankruptcy and reorganization. Frank Wilson, Chief of the US Secret Service in the 1930s, is considered to be the father of forensic accounting. He put an end to Al Capone's criminal career by inspecting his financial reporting and taking him to court for tax evasion. Since then, forensic accountants have been trained and employed with accounting firms everywhere. They often specialise in typical areas, such as insurance and personal injury claims, construction, or royalties.

1	fraud	a	Geldwäsche
2	white collar crime	b	Restrukturierung
3	bribery	c	Wertpapiere
4	embezzlement	d	Personenschaden
5	money laundering	e	Lizenzgebühr
6	securities	f	Betrug
7	bankruptcy	g	Untreue
8	reorganisation	h	Wirtschaftskriminalität
9	personal injury	i	Bestechung
10	royalty	j	Insolvenz

 4 What do you know about the structure of auditor reports? Read a brief summary and discuss the questions with a partner.

> An auditor's report (also auditor's opinion or report of public accounting firm) has three main parts: it begins by saying who has been audited for a given period. Then it mentions the financial reporting and auditing standards applied. Finally, it states whether the audited statements present a true and fair view of the audited company's financial position.

1 Which standards for financial reporting and auditing are mentioned in such reports in the UK, the US and Germany?
2 Can public accountants be held liable for not identifying irregularities and falsely attesting to the reasonableness of financial statements? What are the consequences they may face?
3 How do you become a public accountant in your country? What are the requirements and how long does it take?

DID YOU KNOW?

The English terms **audit** and **auditor** are much more general than the very specific German *Wirtschaftsprüfung* and *Wirtschaftsprüfer*in*. You can conduct audits in many fields, such as quality management and IT. Auditing financial statements assumes a public role reserved for members of professional accounting institutions who passed a qualifying exam. In this context, it is much clearer when you add the word **public** and refer to a **public auditor** or **public accountant**. Here are some key English/German terms:

- **public auditing/accounting,** → Wirtschaftsprüfung, Wirtschaftsprüfer*in
  public auditor/accountant
- **external auditing, external auditor** → Buchprüfung, Buchprüfer*in
- **internal auditing, internal auditor** → innere Revision, Revisor*in
- **statutory audit, statutory auditor** → Abschlussprüfung, Abschlussprüfer*in
- **management accounting,** → Controlling, Controller*in
  management accountant

5 MEDIATION

Explain the following overview in plain English to people working outside accounting.

Internal and external auditing: Two distinct processes
Internal and external auditing are used to assess and evaluate financial and operational activities and are crucial for transparency, accountability, and compliance.

Internal auditing
→ independent, objective assurance and consulting activity
→ designed to add value and improve operations
→ focus on internal controls, risk management, and operational efficiency
→ examining processes and systems to ensure compliance
→ carried out by employees who report to the audit committee or senior management and provide recommendations for improvement to enhance performance

External auditing
→ independent examination of financial information
→ forms an opinion to provide assurance to external stakeholders, such as investors and creditors, regarding the accuracy and reliability of the financial statements
→ focus on financial statements and related disclosures
→ ensuring that financial statements reflect a true and fair view of financial position and performance
→ carried out by independent professionals who report to shareholders or regulatory authorities

---

🔊 **6** Listen to a presentation on creative accounting and complete
11   the exercises below.

a **Match the following terms with their definitions.**

1 creative accounting
2 revenue recognition
3 expenses deferral
4 special purpose entity
5 corporate governance

a moving to another, later accounting period
b a company that is set up for a specific aim
c making figures look better than they actually are
d a framework for managing and monitoring companies
e recording items when they are earned

> **VOCABULARY**
>
> to **cook the books** Bücher frisieren
> to **defer sth** etw. verlagern
> to **exploit so/sth** jmdn./etw. ausnutzen
> **fraud** Betrug
> to **inflate sth** etw. aufblähen
> **loophole** Schlupfloch
> to **mask sth** etw. verschleiern
> to **misrepresent sth** etw. falsch darstellen
> to **recognise sth** *hier:* etw. realisieren
> **remuneration** Vergütung

 b **Discuss the concept of special purpose entities/vehicles in more detail. Are they common in your country? How are they regulated?**

 c **With a partner, pick one of the following cases and use the internet to find out about the creative accounting methods employed. Then present your findings.**

- Tobashi scheme
- Investment bank Lehman Brothers' Repo 105 scheme
- Italian dairy company Parmalat (the largest bankruptcy in European history)
- Investment bank Goldman Sachs & the Greek debt crisis
- Sportswear company Nike & its Swoosh logo offshoring

USEFUL PHRASES   Describing trends and developments

▲
- There has been a **sharp increase** in prices.
- We have seen a **significant rise** in turnover.
- Sales **shot up** after last year's update.
- Order numbers **skyrocketed** when a new version was announced.
- They **reached a peak** in March.

▼
- Profits **decreased slightly**.
- Figures **gradually fell** over the last years and **bottomed out** in 2025.
- The share price **slumped** when the CEO resigned.
- Bonus payments **plunged** due to poor performance.
- They **hit a low** in 2025.

—
- Prices **were stable** in the last quarter.
- The tax burden **remained steady** at 25%.
- Corporate taxation **stayed the same** in the last ten years.

~
- Tax rates **fluctuated** considerably, but **recovered**.

If you want to link effect to cause:
- The loss was **caused by** balance sheet adjustments.

If you want to link cause to effect:
- Balance sheet adjustments **led to** a loss.

> **Presentations** should have a **clear structure** and **appropriate language**. After you have **welcomed** your audience, **introduce** yourself (and any co-presenters) and your topic. Then, give an **overview** of the items you will cover using **signposts** (cf. Useful Phrases, p. 24). Once you have covered your items, **summarise** and come to a conclusion. Invite **questions**.

VOCABULARY

to **plunge** abstürzen
to **reach a peak** einen Höchststand erreichen
to **skyrocket** hochschnellen
to **slump** einbrechen

7 Presentations often include charts. Label them with words from the box.

bar chart | line graph | pie chart | table

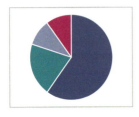 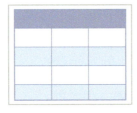 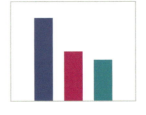 

1 _____ 2 _____ 3 _____ 4 _____

a Draw a graph based on the following description.

"I'd like you to look at the graph, which shows the development of sales in the last year. As you can see, sales rose steadily from €7m during the first quarter. They reached a peak at €10m at the end of March. Then, they slightly dropped to €9m in April. They remained steady over the next three months before falling to €5m in August. They fluctuated between September and November, but recovered in December, closing at €8m."

b Pick a listed company of your choice, access its chart on a financial market's website (e.g. Wallstreet Online, Yahoo Finance, Baha), and describe the development of its share price over the last ten years.

ENGLISH FOR TAX PROFESSIONALS

8 Companies not only report on financial matters. Reporting on sustainability is an integral part of many annual reports. Discuss in class what aspects of sustainability are addressed, and why stakeholders might be interested in them.

9 Read the following text on the EU Green Deal and complete the task below.

> Making Europe the first climate-neutral continent in the world is a binding commitment under EU climate laws. As part of the EU Green Deal, companies are required to report not only on financial matters, but also on sustainability. They must provide information on the risks and opportunities they see arising from social and environmental issues, including the impact of their activities on people and the environment.
>
> This entails:
> - environmental matters
> - social matters and treatment of employees
> - respect for human rights
> - anti-corruption and bribery
> - diversity on company boards in terms of age, gender, educational and professional background
>
> This is aimed at helping investors, civil society organisations, consumers and other stakeholders to evaluate the sustainability performance of companies.

With a partner, do research on those parts of EU legislation that govern non-financial reporting (regulations, directives, standards). Consider the questions below and present your findings in class.

1 What type of companies are required to report under the EU Green Deal? Explain the criteria applied (size, sales, etc).
2 Do companies have to provide this information separately or included in annual reports? Why?

VOCABULARY

commitment Verpflichtung
directive Richtlinie
regulation Verordnung
sustainability reporting
 Nachhaltigkeitsberichterstattung

*A **stakeholder** is not just a shareholder, but anyone interested in a company's affairs, including staff, customers, suppliers, media, government authorities and the scientific community.*
*The **Corporate Sustainability Reporting Directive** (**CSRD**) requires companies to report on sustainability according to the **European Sustainability Reporting Standards** (**ESRS**).*

10 Which of the following ESG reporting items belong to environmental (E), social (S), or governance categories (G)? Check the ESRS online and decide which standards are met by these items.

- board composition
- headcount
- greenhouse gas emissions
- employee turnover
- waste management
- audit committee
- gender diversity
- lost time incidents

*The **audit committee** is responsible for overseeing the financial reporting process, selecting auditors and receiving audit results.*

***Lost time incidents** (**LTI**) are accidents that result in time off from work.*

***Employee** (or **staff**) **turnover** is the percentage of employees that leave a company during a reporting period.*

UNIT 6: WORKING IN AUDITING

DID YOU KNOW?

EU legislation mainly consists of regulations and directives. While **regulations**, such as the General Data Protection Regulation (GDPR) apply directly in all member states, **directives**, such as the Corporate Sustainability Reporting Directive (CSRD) must be implemented by each member state through national legislation. This process is called **transposition** (verb: to transpose), which is a special term not used in standard English.
EU English ("Eurospeak") has an array of rather uncommon expressions and uses. For example, **agent** can stand for "employee", **delay** for "deadline", and **retain** for "choose". There are even "creations" such as **decommit** (cancel), **hierarchical superior** (boss), or **planification** (planning). So be careful with Eurospeak in a non-EU context.

11 SIMULATION

A company invites you to give a presentation on the topic of auditor liability. Team up with two other members of your class and share the preparation and delivery. Divide the items below among yourselves.

- Do an internet search to find out what various institutions such as the Association of Chartered Certified Accountants (ACCA) and the European Commission say about auditor liability.
- Take notes on the types of liability (criminal/civil/public), its scope, exclusion and limitation options by law or arrangement, as well as possible sanctions.
- Draw a comparison to the situation in your country and the regulations in force.
- Illustrate your findings by giving examples of actual cases.

Refer to the Useful Phrases on pages 24 and 50 to structure your presentation. Introduce any co-presenter that follows you as topics shift. Include a Q&A slot at the end to accommodate the other members of your class, who will assume the role of company representatives.

12 Do you know the correct English terms for these false friends? Write them on the line.

Daten	dates	
Formular	formula	
Gratifikation	gratification	
Konzern	concern	
Muttergesellschaft	mother company	
Protokoll	protocol	
Provision	provision	
Quote	quote	
Rate	rate	
Steuererklärung	tax declaration	
Tochtergesellschaft	daughter company	
übernehmen	to overtake	

*There are many English words in other languages with the same meaning as in English. Such **true friends** include words such as "audit", "cash flow", "compliance", "corporate governance", "due diligence", and many more.*
***False friends**, on the other hand, are to be avoided as they may resemble or even look the same, but have another meaning.*

OVER TO YOU

Lessons learned from Wirecard?

Several accounting scandals have become known over the years, but cases still keep coming. A famous one in recent history was German blue chip company Wirecard: a major financial services provider and fintech star on the stock exchange that went bankrupt. They had almost € 2bn in their books that did not exist, and more than € 3bn debts that they left behind. Several managers faced criminal charges, and the company's COO went into hiding at an unknown place.

When the news came out, the share price plunged, and investors lost a lot of money. A company once worth billions, employing more than 5,000 people, was just hot air. But besides this, the role of supervisory bodies came into question. Why have they failed? Why was it possible to cook the books for so many years without anyone noticing? Wirecard's directors and auditors were regularly discharged at AGMs. Its own supervisory board did not question anything despite ongoing media reporting.

The European Securities and Markets Authority (ESMA) concluded that German watchdogs such as BaFin "failed completely". Shareholders claimed damages, and a € 500,000 fine was imposed on Wirecard's accounting firm for having breached their duties. They were also banned from auditing major companies for two years.

So what are the lessons learned? Without a doubt, people, governments and the media are on high alert. Laws have been changed, supervisory powers enhanced, rules tightened. So are accounting scandals history now? We will see.

VOCABULARY

AGM (annual general meeting) Jahreshauptversammlung
to be on high alert in hoher Alarmbereitschaft sein
to breach sth etw. verletzen
COO (Chief Operating Officer) Vorstand für das operative Geschäft
damages (pl.) Schadensersatz
to discharge *hier:* entlasten
to go into hiding untertauchen
fine Bußgeld
supervisory board Aufsichtsrat
supervisory body/watchdog Aufsichtsbehörde
to tighten *hier:* verschärfen

1 Has the Wirecard case come to a conclusion? What are the results for its investors, directors and auditors?
2 Do you know other cases where auditors have been fined, or banned from working? Why does it often prove difficult to hold them liable?
3 Are you aware of other accounting scandals that shook the industry?

> **BaFin** (Bundesanstalt für Finanzdienstleistungen) is the German financial markets watchdog. The regulatory authority for auditors is **APAS** (Abschlussprüferaufsichtsstelle). It conducts independent inspections and investigates cases of professional misconduct.

MATERIALS

UNIT 3   Exercise 7

Anlage EÜR

Betriebsausgabenpauschale **für bestimmte Berufsgruppen**

Sachlicher Bebauungskostenrichtbetrag und Ausbaukostenrichtbeträge für **Weinbaubetriebe**
(Übertrag aus Zeile 12 der Anlage LuF)

Betriebsausgabenpauschale für **Forstwirte** (Übertrag aus Zeile 16 der Anlage LuF)

Waren, Rohstoffe und Hilfsstoffe einschl. der Nebenkosten

Bezogene Fremdleistungen

Ausgaben für eigenes Personal (z. B. Gehälter, Löhne und Versicherungsbeiträge)

Absetzung für Abnutzung (AfA)

AfA auf unbewegliche Wirtschaftsgüter (Übertrag aus Zeile 6 der Anlage AVEÜR)

AfA auf immaterielle Wirtschaftsgüter (Übertrag aus Zeile 9 der Anlage AVEÜR)

AfA auf bewegliche Wirtschaftsgüter (Übertrag aus Zeile 13 der Anlage AVEÜR)

Sonderabschreibungen nach § 7b EStG und § 7g Abs. 5 und 6 EStG
(Übertrag der Summe der Zeilen 4 und 13 der Anlage AVEÜR)

Herabsetzungsbeträge nach § 7g Abs. 2 Satz 3 EStG
(Erläuterungen auf gesondertem Blatt)

Aufwendungen für geringwertige Wirtschaftsgüter nach § 6 Abs. 2 EStG

Auflösung Sammelposten nach § 6 Abs. 2a EStG (Übertrag aus Zeile 19 der Anlage AVEÜR)

Restbuchwert der ausgeschiedenen Anlagegüter
(Übertrag der Summe der Einzelbeträge aus Spalte „Abgänge" der Anlage AVEÜR ohne Zeile 22)

Raumkosten und sonstige Grundstücksaufwendungen
(ohne häusliches Arbeitszimmer)
Miete/Pacht für Geschäftsräume und betrieblich genutzte Grundstücke

Aufwendungen für doppelte Haushaltsführung (z. B. Miete)

Sonstige Aufwendungen für betrieblich genutzte Grundstücke
(ohne Schuldzinsen und AfA)

Sonstige unbeschränkt abziehbare Betriebsausgaben

Aufwendungen für Telekommunikation (z. B. Telefon, Internet)

Übernachtungs- und Reisenebenkosten bei Geschäftsreisen des Steuerpflichtigen

Fortbildungskosten (ohne Reisekosten)

Kosten für Rechts- und Steuerberatung, Buchführung

Miete/Leasing für bewegliche Wirtschaftsgüter (ohne Kraftfahrzeuge)

Erhaltungsaufwendungen (z. B. Instandhaltung, Wartung, Reparatur; ohne solche für Gebäude und Kraftfahrzeuge)

Beiträge, Gebühren, Abgaben und Versicherungen (ohne solche für Gebäude und Kraftfahrzeuge)

Laufende EDV-Kosten (z. B. Beratung, Wartung, Reparatur)

Arbeitsmittel (z. B. Bürobedarf, Porto, Fachliteratur)

Kosten für Abfallbeseitigung und Entsorgung

Kosten für Verpackung und Transport

Werbekosten (z. B. Inserate, Werbespots, Plakate)

Schuldzinsen zur Finanzierung von Anschaffungs- und Herstellungskosten von Wirtschaftsgütern des Anlagevermögens (ohne häusliches Arbeitszimmer)

Übrige Schuldzinsen

Gezahlte Vorsteuerbeträge

An das Finanzamt gezahlte und ggf. verrechnete Umsatzsteuer
(Die Regelung zum 10-Tageszeitraum nach § 11 Abs. 2 Satz 2 EStG ist zu beachten.)

Rücklagen, stille Reserven und/oder Ausgleichsposten (Übertrag aus Zeile 124)

Übrige unbeschränkt abziehbare Betriebsausgaben
(auch zurückgezahlte Hilfen/Zuschüsse aufgrund der Corona-Pandemie)

Beschränkt abziehbare Betriebsausgaben

	nicht abziehbar EUR / Ct		abziehbar EUR / Ct
Geschenke	164	174	
Bewirtungsaufwendungen	165	175	
Verpflegungsmehraufwendungen		171	
Aufwendungen für ein häusliches Arbeitszimmer (einschl. AfA und Schuldzinsen)	162	172	
Sonstige beschränkt abziehbare Betriebsausgaben	168	177	

Kraftfahrzeugkosten und andere Fahrtkosten

Leasingkosten

Steuern, Versicherungen und Maut

Sonstige tatsächliche Fahrtkosten ohne AfA und Zinsen (z. B. Reparaturen, Wartungen, Treibstoff, Kosten für Flugstrecken, Kosten für öffentliche Verkehrsmittel)

Fahrtkosten für nicht zum Betriebsvermögen gehörende Fahrzeuge (Nutzungseinlage)

Fahrtkosten für Wege zwischen Wohnung und erster Betriebsstätte; Familienheimfahrten
(pauschaliert oder tatsächlich)

Mindestens abziehbare Fahrtkosten für Wege zwischen Wohnung und erster Betriebsstätte
(Entfernungspauschale); Familienheimfahrten

(*Bundesministerium der Finanzen*)

MATERIALS

UNIT 4   Exercise 12

XYZ, INC.
BALANCE SHEET
(in million US dollars)

	December 31,	
	2028	2029
ASSETS		
Current assets:		
Cash and cash equivalents	$ 36,220	$ 53,888
Marketable securities	59,829	16,138
Inventories	32,640	34,405
Accounts receivable, net and other	32,891	42,360
Total current assets	161,580	146,791
Property and equipment, net	160,281	186,715
Operating leases	56,082	66,123
Goodwill	15,371	20,288
Other assets	27,235	42,758
Total assets	$ 420,549	$ 462,675
LIABILITIES AND STOCKHOLDERS' EQUITY		
Current liabilities:		
Accounts payable	$ 78,664	$ 79,600
Accrued expenses and other	51,775	62,566
Unearned revenue	11,827	13,227
Total current liabilities	142,266	155,393
Long-term lease liabilities	67,651	72,968
Long-term debt	48,744	67,150
Other long-term liabilities	23,643	21,121
Stockholders' equity	138,245	146,043
Total liabilities and stockholders' equity	$ 420,549	$ 462,675

STATEMENT OF INCOME (LOSS)
(in million US dollars)

	Year Ended December 31,		
	2027	2028	2029
Net income (loss)	$ 21,331	$ 33,364	$ (2,722)

TRANSCRIPTS

UNIT 1   Exercise 7

🔊 02

Martin: Ms Croud, isn't it? My name is Schmidt, Martin Schmidt.
Jane: Nice to meet you.
Martin: If you'd like to follow me to my office, please … Is this your first visit to Emden, Ms Croud?
Jane: Yes, it is, and I like it very much. I've had the chance to look around a bit before coming to your office. I retired last year and decided to move to Borkum after working in Saxony for many years.
Martin: You've certainly chosen the right place.
Jane: Borkum is a wonderful island, it's just wonderful.
Martin: Where are you from originally?
Jane: I'm from Wales.
Martin: Another beautiful place. …
So, this is my office. Please have a seat, Ms Croud. May I offer you a cup of tea?
Jane: I'd love one.
Martin: With milk?
Jane: Of course …. oh, and you even have real milk, what a treat! I was at a café the other day, and I had to put evaporated milk in my tea. Terrible.
Martin: We do what we can, Ms Croud. I understand you spent quite some time in Germany and decided to stay?
Jane: Yes, that's right. Almost 20 years. My husband passed away last year, and we spent holidays in many different places in Germany. I just love Borkum, so I chose it as my "final destination". Sylt is nice, too – but with my pension and the taxes I might have to pay, I think I'll have a better life on Borkum. Which brings me to my question: I understand my pension will be taxed?
Martin: Well, only a certain portion of your pension is taxable. Since when have you been getting your pension?
Jane: 2024. It's € 1,800 a month.
Martin: I see … that's € 21,600 a year. 84% of that amount is taxable … that's € 18,144. From this amount you can deduct health and care insurance contributions and certain allowances: € 102 for income-related and € 36 for special expenses. I assume you'll end up with a taxable amount of about € 15,000.
Jane: And how much of that will go to the government?
Martin: Well, you'll have to pay taxes on the amount exceeding € 11,604 … roughly € 500 – and you'll have to file a tax return.
Jane: OK. € 500 a year won't kill me. Thank you.
Martin: Let me know if there's anything else I can do for you – and have a wonderful time on Borkum!

UNIT 2   Exercise 2

🔊 03

Assistant: Steuerberater Meister, Goldschmidt, Guten Tag.
Client: Sorry, do you speak English?
Assistant: Certainly. What can I do for you?
Client: I'd like to make an appointment to see a tax advisor.
Assistant: Can I ask what it's about?
Client: Yes, I'm just starting a job in Germany next month, and I'd like to get information on taxes and social security.
Assistant: I see. Let me just check the diary. Please hold.
…
Thank you for holding. Would Tuesday at 3 o'clock suit you?
Client: I'm afraid that's not convenient for me.
Assistant: OK. What about Wednesday at 9 a.m. then?
Client: That would work for me.
Assistant: May I have your name, please?
Client: It's Blair, John Blair.
Assistant: And may I have your phone number, Mr Blair?
Client: Of course. It's 0162 2082784.
Assistant: Ok, Mr Blair, I've scheduled you for Wednesday at 9 o'clock. Mr Meister will take care of you. Is there anything else I can do for you?
Client: Could you give me the full address, please?
Assistant: Of course. It's Kanzleistr. 20. Please refer to our website for directions.
Client: Oh, great. Could you give me that address too?
Assistant: Sure. Let me spell that for you: it's w-w-w dot s-t-b minus t-h-o-m-a-s minus m-e-i-s-t-e-r dot d-e slash directions.
Client: Okay … can I just read that back to you: w-w-w dot s-t-b minus t-h-o-m-a-s minus m-e-i-s-t-e-r dot d-e slash directions?
Assistant: That's correct.
Client: Well, thanks a lot. One last question: How much will I have to pay for your service?
Assistant: At our firm, we charge € 150 plus VAT for an initial consultation. Is that acceptable to you?
Client: I think so. See you on Wednesday.
Assistant: Thank you for calling. Good-bye, Mr Blair.

TRANSCRIPTS

UNIT 2   Exercise 5

 04

Thomas: Well, there are two factors you have to consider: social security contributions and income tax. Both are deducted at source.
John: This means I don't have to pay them myself, but my employer does it for me?
Thomas: Exactly. Social security has four tiers: pension, unemployment, health and care insurance. These add up to roughly 40% of your salary, but half of it is paid by your employer. In effect, about 20% of your gross income will be social security deductions.
John: Can I choose the pension and health insurance myself?
Thomas: Well, not quite. There is only one single state pension, so you have no choice there, but there are many different state health insurance schemes. You can choose that yourself and let your employer know which one you have chosen.
John: Is there anything I have to bear in mind when choosing health insurance?
Thomas: Not really. Most cover the same. There are minor differences when it comes to service and incentives. You could check the internet for a comparison. There's a uniform rate, but insurers may levy a surcharge.
John: I've heard that private cover is much better. Can I opt for one?
Thomas: I'm afraid you can't. You'd need to be above a certain income threshold. At the moment, you don't have a choice.
John: I see. What about taxes?
Thomas: Well, they depend on your income and your family situation. Are you married?
John: I'm single.
Thomas: Do you have any children?
John: No, I don't.
Thomas: Ok. In this case you have a tax-free allowance of about € 12,000, but in fact your employer will only deduct taxes on income exceeding € 15,000. This is due to the fact that certain additional allowances are automatically taken into account. Let's see … you'll earn € 36,000 a year, so you can expect to pay about 20% income tax.
John: … so 20% tax plus 20% social security deductions … 40% from € 3,000 is 3,6,9 … 1,200 … so I'll have …
Thomas: … € 1,800 net.
John: Ah, that's good to know. I have one last question: do I have to file a tax return? I've heard my employer does it electronically.

Thomas: Your employer will forward your income details to your tax office, and you'll get a receipt with a reference number. As long as you don't have any other income, you don't have to file a return, but it could be advisable as you often get a refund. I'd be happy to assist you.
John: Certainly, especially if you can help me to minimize my tax burden.
Thomas: I'll do all I can. Please feel free to make an appointment with me whenever the need arises.
John: Thank you. I'll be in touch. Good-bye.
Thomas: Have a good start here. Good-bye, Mr Blair.

UNIT 3   Exercise 1

 05

Thomas: Good morning. Nice to see you again.
John: Hello, Mr Meister.
Thomas: It's been quite a while since we last met.
John: Yes, that's right. About three years.
Thomas: So how is life in Germany?
John: Not too bad. I've got used to many things, and really like my neighbourhood - the whole city actually.
Thomas: I'm happy to hear that! And how is work?
John: It has gone quite well so far, but my employer is going to reduce my workload and put me on a 25-hour contract. That's the reason I'm here. I'd like to earn some extra money to make up for the lost income. I thought I could give some English lessons. I've already talked to a few language schools, and they would be happy to hire me.
Thomas: I see. There are a variety of things you'll have to do in connection with taxes. First, you'll have to inform your tax office. There is a special form to be filled in with questions about your type of work and your expected turnover. Then you'll have to prepare invoices that match certain criteria. For example, you'll have to include your tax number and assign invoice numbers. I'll send you details and a sample invoice.
John: Thank you. Will I have to charge VAT?
Thomas: That depends. If your turnover exceeds € 22,000, you'll have to charge it. But you can opt for charging it anyway, independent of your turnover.
John: Would that make sense?
Thomas: In your case, probably not. The advantage of charging VAT is that you can deduct the VAT you pay on goods and services bought for your business from your VAT burden. So it certainly is advantageous when you incur significant expenses, for example a car, office space rent and equipment. In the end, VAT is a transitory item: you'll pass on the VAT you collect to your tax office on a monthly or quarterly basis.

ENGLISH FOR TAX PROFESSIONALS

John: I don't think I'll make a lot of money. From what I've heard, teaching is not paid very well. It's basically to make up for the lost hours and the salary cut involved. Can I actually deduct the rent I pay for my flat?
Thomas: Well, if you were working full-time as a freelancer and your flat was 75sq.m. and the room you were using as your office was 25sq.m., you could deduct an appropriate fraction of the rent as a business expense, in this case one third, plus the corresponding costs for heating and electricity. But only if the tax office accepts that you have dedicated space at home.
John: Well that sounds good.
Thomas: Why don't you give me a call once you're about to start, and we can then discuss what needs to be done. I'll send you a link to a questionnaire that we'll have to work on.
John: That's a good idea. Thank you. Are there any deadlines to observe?
Thomas: Well, once you've finally decided to go freelance and have your first client lined up, you'll have a month to submit the registration form to your tax office. You also need to do that to get a tax number for your invoices. No tax number, no invoice, no money.
John: I see. I'll be in touch. Thanks very much indeed.

UNIT 3   Exercise 3

🔊 06

Thomas: So, Mr Blair, which parts of the form shall we talk about?
John: Well, I've been able to work out some of it myself. But I have trouble with items 3, 4 and 7. Let me just share my screen.
Thomas: OK. Let's do this step by step. Item 3 is about advance payments on your future income tax. You are asked to estimate your turnover for this and for next year. Have you already thought about this?
John: Yes, I have. As I'll only teach part time, I expect around €6,000 this year, and if things go well, maybe €8,000 next year.
Thomas: Fine. You can put these figures in the first and the third column on the third line under 3.1, where it says "Selbständiger Arbeit". But you should consider some expenses you'll incur, maybe a thousand euros. So go for €5,000 and €7,000, respectively.
John: So the first column for this year?
Thomas: That's correct.
John: Got that.

Thomas: Great. Let's move on to item number 4. This is about how you will calculate your profit. You have two options: drafting a balance sheet or cash accounting.
John: What would you recommend?
Thomas: In your case, it doesn't make sense to go the hard way. Cash accounting will do. It's simply "turnover minus expenses".
John: So it's like a profit and loss account?
Thomas: Exactly. It's called "Einnahmenüberschuss-rechnung". It will reflect the money you received and the surplus you made after you deducted expenses.
John: I see four options here.
Thomas: Don't bother about them. Only 1 and 2 are relevant for you, so enter number 1.
John: OK. Done. 7 is next.
Thomas: Very important. Enter your expected turnover here. Year one, then year two. In light of your expected earnings, and also your low expenses, I'd avoid VAT. It would just cost you extra time and effort with no benefit attached. As long as you don't get more than €22,000 a year, you can call yourself a "Kleinunternehmer", a small entrepreneur, and stay away from VAT.
John: It would also make me more expensive, wouldn't it?
Thomas: Certainly when it comes to private clients. They cannot deduct VAT. The same applies to some associations, clubs and schools. Be careful here: tick the first box under item number 7.3. If you tick the other one, you'll have to charge VAT for at least five years.
John: Gosh. Don't want that. OK. 7.8 and we're done. What's this? "Shall" and "is" taxation ... doesn't say anything to me.
Thomas: This doesn't apply to you as you have chosen not to charge VAT. If you did, you'd have to file extra returns and opt for paying VAT as invoiced or collected. But this will become relevant should you ever go over the turnover limit.
John: Fine. That's it I guess. Hard work – I need a rest now.
Thomas: Happy resting, Mr Blair. And remember you have to submit this electronically.
John: I will, I will. Bye for now.

UNIT 4   Exercise 1

🔊 07

Anna: Hello, Mr Dudziak. I'm Anna Springer.
Alexander: I'm Alexander. Nice to meet you.
Tim: Tim. Pleased to meet you.
Anna: Nice to meet you, too. Can I offer you something to drink?

TRANSCRIPTS

Tim: Not for me, thanks.
Alexander: A glass of water, please.
Anna: Still or sparkling?
Alexander: Still, please.
...
Anna: Here you are.
Alexander: Thank you.
Anna: You're welcome. I understand you are here to discuss a start-up matter with me?
Alexander: That's right. Me and my brother would like to do some business in the telecommunications field. We'll be moving to Berlin in a few months, and we were thinking of running a mobile phone sales shop. We have already done that in Poland, and we believe it can be good business in Germany too. From what I've read on the internet there are several forms of businesses we could opt for. Could you give us some information on the options and the different kinds of taxes involved?
Anna: Sure. There are two basic structures: partnerships and corporations. In partnerships, every partner is taxed individually, whereas corporations are taxed as an entity. Depending on the form of business you choose, you will have to deal with VAT, trade and corporation tax. You only have to worry about corporation tax if you decide to operate as a corporation, that means as a limited company.
Tim: What is the tax rate?
Anna: It's 15%. Then there is trade tax, levied on profits of trading businesses. It's quite complicated to explain how it's calculated, and it also depends on the town where your business is located. If you are in a partnership, there is a tax-free allowance of € 24,500.
Tim: So this means that if our profit doesn't exceed this amount, we won't pay any trade tax at all?
Anna: That's right.
Alexander: Well, we're hoping to make more than that, so I don't think we'd end up paying nothing! You also mentioned VAT?
Anna: Yes, that's right. You'll have to charge your customers VAT and file quarterly or monthly VAT returns. You'll pass on the VAT you have collected to your tax office. So VAT is an ongoing issue, whereas trade and corporation tax are assessed yearly. But our tax officers want to have advance payments during the year on those two taxes.
Tim: Yes, they always seem to be asking for something.
Alexander: One more question: I've heard that there's also something like a "church tax" in Germany? I find that very strange. Is this relevant for running a business, too?

Anna: Well, church tax is a personal tax that you pay if you are a member of a registered church. It's calculated as a percentage of the income tax that a person pays and amounts to between eight and nine per cent of the income tax sum.
Alexander: With all these different taxes to consider, I have to say that I'm a bit confused. What business form would you choose?
Anna: That's difficult to say. When you compare the taxation of partnerships and corporations, I can tell you that the difference isn't significant and may add up to around 6%. You'll have to consider not only tax, but also legal and economic aspects. Liability might be an issue. Or the trading volume. There's so much to consider that we should leave it for another talk. Let me prepare something and send to you. Then you can consider the options and we can have another meeting.
Tim: That sounds great. Thank you very much for your assistance.

UNIT 5   Exercise 1

 08

Huan: Hello everybody, thank you very much for joining. We are here to discuss VAT issues in connection with our export/import business with countries in the European Union. We are joined today by our German subsidiary's tax consultant, Ms Luise Ganter. Good afternoon, Ms Ganter.
Luise: Good morning. Good to see you all.
Huan: Ms Ganter, we have Mr Mahmoud Al Khatib from Cairo, and Ms Marcia Amaral from Buenos Aires with us. We have been wondering about proper VAT accounting in our dealings with EU and non-EU countries. Mahmoud, could you please explain your situation?
Mahmoud: Of course. Thank you for this opportunity. We have found a new supplier based in Romania. We would like to have this company supply directly to customers in France where we have no business of our own. I know that we normally have to register for VAT where our customers are based. Maybe there is a better way?
Luise: Well, there is a mechanism in EU trade called triangulation. This is a chain of supplies of goods involving three parties when, instead of the goods physically passing from one party to the next, they are delivered directly from the first party to the last in the chain.
Marcia: I'm sorry, I don't quite understand. Could you give me an example?

ENGLISH FOR TAX PROFESSIONALS

Luise: Of course. Mahmoud said you have a Romanian company sending goods directly to your French customer. If you let your German company handle these orders, you won't have to bother with VAT.
Marcia: How come?
Luise: The German company receives an order from a French company and sources the goods from a Romanian company, which sends the goods directly to the French customer. The French pays the German, and the German pays the Romanian company.
Mahmoud: And then?
Luise: VAT triangulation rules allow the Romanian company to declare the transaction as an intra-Community supply, the French as an intra-Community acquisition. The German company has no VAT obligations.
Mahmoud: I see. So could any company supply goods under similar arrangements throughout the EU without having to register in every member state?
Luise: As long as the three companies involved are all in the EU, yes. Triangulation was introduced to simplify EU trade and avoid the hassle of registering everywhere.
Huan: What if more than three companies were involved?
Luise: No simplification would be possible then.
Huan: And what if our Argentinian colleagues got an order?
Marcia: Thank you, Huan. I wanted to ask the same question. Let's say it's not Germany, but us who receive an order from a customer in the EU and let a supplier from another member state send goods directly to our customer.
Luise: If you are not registered for VAT within the EU, the Romanian company will make a VAT inclusive supply.
Marcia: At what rate?
Luise: At the appropriate Romanian VAT rate.
Marcia: And if we were registered for VAT in France?
Luise: Then, the Romanian trader would zero-rate the goods for VAT and declare them as a supply.
Mahmoud: And what happens when you are registered for VAT in another EU country?
Luise: Then you can simplify and take advantage of the triangulation regime.
Huan: It seems to me that we should let our German business handle all trade within the European Union. This will reduce red tape and save us a lot of work and time. And time is money.
Mahmoud: I'd agree and say the simpler the better. But let us think about it and discuss this at another meeting. What do you think?
Marcia: Sounds good to me.

Huan: OK then, this has been really helpful. Thank you all for your contributions. And thank you, Ms Ganter, for answering our questions. Good-bye.

UNIT 5   Exercise 5

 09

Countries typically tax income based on either residence or source. Residence means that you are taxed on your worldwide income, source involves being taxed where you earn your money. Most countries apply the 183-day rule, which means you are considered resident and taxable in a country when you spend more than half a year in it.
For businesses, the concept of permanent establishment is key. It is a fixed place of business with a sufficient presence in a country to be subject to taxation.
Double taxation occurs when the same income is taxed in more than one country. Countries often enter into double taxation agreements to avoid this. They provide tax credits that offset taxes you owe in your home country, or tax exemptions that exclude certain types of foreign income from taxation.
Tax avoidance refers to legal methods to minimize taxes. Tax evasion, on the other hand, involves illegal activities. While tax avoidance is lawful, it can be controversial, as it may be perceived as exploiting loopholes. A special area is transfer pricing, involving transactions between related entities (e.g. group companies). These must in line with fair market prices to prevent profit shifting and tax avoidance by trading on favourable terms. Tax havens are a particular concern in terms of fair taxation. Companies use strategies to exploit gaps and mismatches in tax rules to artificially shift profits to low or no-tax locations. This is known as base erosion and profit shifting.

UNIT 6   Exercise 2

10

EA: The last time we met, I pointed out a few critical items in connection with your internal controls. I'd like to discuss any significant changes since my last audit.
IA: Sure. We've made some updates to our internal controls in the past year to enhance efficiency and address identified weaknesses. Shall I walk you through those changes?

TRANSCRIPTS

EA: That would be great. Let's start with the general control environment. Have there been any modifications or improvements to the company's overall control framework?

IA: Yes, we've implemented a more robust control framework to align with industry best practices. We've also conducted training sessions to ensure that all employees are aware of their roles in maintaining internal controls.

EA: Excellent. Now, let's dive into specific controls. Have there been any changes to the authorization and approval processes for financial transactions?

IA: We've revised our approval workflows to add an additional layer of review for high-value transactions. This has helped us prevent any potential errors or fraudulent activities.

EA: That sounds like a positive step. How about the information technology controls? Have there been any updates to the systems, and how are you ensuring the security of financial data?

IA: We've invested in upgrading our IT infrastructure to enhance data security. We've also implemented multi-factor authentication and regularly conduct penetration testing to identify and address any vulnerabilities.

EA: It's good to see a focus on cybersecurity. Moving on to the financial reporting process, have there been any changes in accounting policies or estimates?

IA: No significant changes in accounting policies, but we have refined our estimation methods based on feedback from the previous audit to ensure greater accuracy in financial reporting.

EA: That's important for maintaining the integrity of financial statements. Lastly, have there been any identified areas of concern or incidents related to fraud or irregularities?

IA: We haven't identified any fraud or irregularities, but we continuously monitor and investigate any suspicious activities. Our whistleblower program also encourages employees to report any concerns anonymously.

EA: Thank you. It seems like your internal control environment is well-maintained and responsive to potential risks. I appreciate your time and the thorough overview of the changes since our last audit.

IA: You're welcome. If you have any further questions during your audit process, feel free to reach out. We want to ensure a smooth audit process.

UNIT 6   Exercise 6

🔊 11   Good morning, everybody. I'm Fatma Behrens, and I'd like to talk about creative accounting. I'll start by defining what creative accounting is. Then, I'll discuss the motivation behind such conduct. Next, I'll present famous cases and their consequences. And finally, I'll offer a conclusion. I'd be happy to take questions at the end. So let's start with a definition. Creative accounting is used to make a company look better and healthier than it actually is. It exploits loopholes in accounting rules to misrepresent figures. "Cooking the books" is another word for it. This is done by recognising revenue prematurely, deferring expenses, overstating inventory, masking or undervaluing liabilities. All of this leads to better results, higher income and equity. What drives such conduct? Well, it's very simple: the better the figures, the better for the market and investors. Good figures affect share prices, bonuses and directors' remuneration.

Let's look at some examples. Enron and WorldCom were once huge companies that went bankrupt after their accounting practices surfaced. Enron used special purpose entities to move debts off their balance sheet, thus inflating their earnings. WorldCom overstated its assets by billions. Executives from both companies ended up in prison. But the consequences have been much vaster, leading to stricter global standards for transparency, corporate governance and financial disclosures. In the US, the Sarbanes-Oxley Act was passed shortly after these scandals, introducing comprehensive measures.

In conclusion, creative accounting poses significant risks. It can lead to fraud, bankruptcy and criminal charges. And it breaches trust with auditors, investors, staff and the general public. At the end of the day, transparency, integrity, and ethical conduct are key.

Thank you for your attention. Now, let's open the floor for any questions or discussions you may have on the topic.

ANSWER KEY

UNIT 1

Warm-up
Sample answers:
- advise landlords on rental income
- advise pensioners on taxation of pensions
- advise investors on capital gains tax
- advise on social security matters
- advise on start-ups
- advise on inheritance matters
- prepare tax returns
- draft financial statements
- represent clients before tax offices and courts
- do payroll accounting
- help with estate planning

Exercise 2
1 represent   2 payroll   3 returns   4 refund
5 corporate   6 VAT   7 start-ups   8 trustees
9 opinions   10 estate   11 fee schedule
12 partnership   13 limited company   14 compete
15 public accountants

Exercise 3
- Auditing
- Giving general legal advice, e.g. on consumer law issues

Exercise 6
2 refund   3 return   4 hike   5 cut   6 allowance
7 incentive   8 deduction   9 assessment   10 bracket

Exercise 7
Meeting & greeting
- Ms Croud, isn't it?
- My name is Schmidt, Martin Schmidt.
- Nice to meet you.

Offering hospitality
- Please have a seat.
- May I offer you a cup of tea?

Small talk
- Is this your first visit to Emden?
- Where are you from originally?
- I understand you spent quite some time in Germany and decided to stay?

Exercise 9
"Which brings me to my question: …"

Exercise 10
a 1 2   2 1   3 2   4 2   5 1

b 1 accounting   2 audit   3 freedom   4 adherence
5 preparation

c 2 h   3 d   4 f   5 a   6 b   7 e   8 c

UNIT 2

Warm-up
1 farming & forestry   2 trade   3 self-employment
4 employment   5 capital assets   6 rental   7 other

5 a   4 b   6 c   3 d   7 e   2 f   5 g   3 h   2 i   2 j

Exercise 1
1 c (–)   2 f (–)   3 g (+)   4 i (–)   5 h (–)   6 j (~)
7 a (–)   8 d (~)   9 e (–)   10 b (–)

Exercise 2
1 2   2 2   3 2   4 1   5 2

1 John wants to make an appointment.
2 0162 2082784
3 www.stb-thomas-meister.de/directions

Exercise 5
a
- 20% social security contributions (John's share)
- 40% social security contributions (total), €
- 1200 tax + social security deductions
- 1800 net income
- 12 000 tax-free allowance
- 15 000 amount from which the employer withholds wage tax
- 36 000 John's annual gross salary

b 1 depend on   2 deduct, exceeding
3 additional allowances   4 expect   5 file
6 receipt, reference   7 refund

c 1 T   2 T   3 F   4 T   5 T

d health insurance, care insurance, unemployment insurance, pension insurance
Fifth pillar: statutory accident insurance, covering work-related accidents

Exercise 7
1 You must file a tax return if you have income from self-employment.
2 If you get/receive interest from your bank, you must pay capital gains tax.
3 If your income-related expenses are low, the tax office automatically applies/considers the higher employee allowance.
4 You can file an appeal within a month if you are unhappy with your tax notice.
5 If you take on a second job/additional employment, it falls into tax bracket 6.

Exercise 9
car insurance, return, claims, tax, alone, withdraw

ANSWER KEY | 63

ANSWER KEY

Exercise 13
1 threshold   2 refund   3 salary   4 assessment
5 bracket   6 appeal   7 bonus   8 logbook
9 return   10 payroll

UNIT 3

Exercise 1
a   1 d   2 c   3 e   4 a   5 b

b   1 hours   2 additional   3 commission   4 meet
5 account for   6 revenue   irrespective
7 subtract   8 costs   9 forward   10 decrease
11 apartment   12 meet

Exercise 3
(see next page)

Exercise 4
1 T   2 F   3 F   4 F

Exercise 7
a *Übrige unbeschränkt abziehbare Betriebsausgaben.*

b Giving a workshop could involve travel
(*Kraftfahrzeugkosten und andere Fahrtkosten*)
accommodation (*Übernachtungs- und
Reisenebenkosten*), and meals (*Verpflegungsmehraufwendungen*).

c Attending a conference could involve fees
(*Fortbildungskosten*), travel (*Kraftfahrzeugkosten
und andere Fahrtkosten*) accommodation
(*Übernachtungs- und Reisenebenkosten*), and meals
(*Verpflegungsmehraufwendungen*).

d *Kraftfahrzeugkosten und andere Fahrtkosten.*

e Only the membership in the teachers' association
is job-related (*Beiträge, Gebühren, Abgaben und
Versicherungen*).

f Only the professional indemnity insurance is
job-related (*Beiträge, Gebühren, Abgaben und
Versicherungen*). The others might be considered
elsewhere (*Sonderausgaben / Vorsorgeaufwand*).

Exercise 8
1 gifts   2 study   3 reserves   4 depreciation
5 intangible assets   6 small-value items
7 maintenance costs   8 debt interest
9 entertainment expenses   10 meal allowance

Exercise 9
2 useful   3 depreciated   4 declining   5 official
6 relief   7 provided   8 choice

Exercise 11
horizontally: invoice, trade, fee, study, bill, VAT
vertically: interest, travel, reserves, insurance,
turnover, depreciation, professional, form, gift,
provision, entertainment
diagonally: debt, sales, profit

I	I	N	V	O	I	C	E	D	G	M	A
N	E	I	E	T	R	A	D	E	E	S	E
T	R	N	V	D	P	I	R	V	A	B	N
E	E	S	C	E	R	R	C	L	N	U	T
R	S	U	T	P	O	S	E	O	V	S	E
E	E	R	U	R	F	S	T	C	S	N	R
S	R	A	R	E	E	F	E	E	S	O	T
T	V	N	N	C	S	T	U	D	Y	I	A
R	E	C	O	I	S	L	N	S	F	S	I
A	S	E	V	A	I	L	M	O	G	I	N
V	E	N	E	T	O	I	R	D	I	V	M
E	U	I	R	I	N	P	O	O	F	O	E
L	L	I	B	O	A	V	F	S	T	R	N
V	A	T	C	N	L	A	R	S	I	P	T

ENGLISH FOR TAX PROFESSIONALS

Exercise 3

Fragebogen zur steuerlichen Erfassung

[X] Aufnahme einer gewerblichen, selbständigen (freiberuflichen) oder land- und forstwirtschaftlichen Tätigkeit

3. Angaben zur Festsetzung der Vorauszahlungen (Einkommensteuer, Gewerbesteuer)

3.1 Voraussichtliche Einkünfte aus	im Jahr der Betriebseröffnung		im Folgejahr	
	Steuerpflichtige(r) EUR	Ehegatte(in)/ Lebenspartner(in) EUR	Steuerpflichtige(r) EUR	Ehegatte(in)/ Lebenspartner(in) EUR
Land- und Forstwirtschaft				
Gewerbebetrieb				
Selbständiger Arbeit	5000		7000	
Nichtselbständiger Arbeit				
Kapitalvermögen				
Vermietung und Verpachtung				
Sonstigen Einkünften (z. B. Renten)				

4. Angaben zur Gewinnermittlung

Gewinnermittlungsart: **1**

1 = Einnahmenüberschussrechnung
2 = Betriebsvermögensvergleich
3 = Gewinnermittlung nach Durchschnittssätzen (nur bei Land- und Forstwirtschaft)
4 = Sonstige (z.B. § 5a EStG) *(Angaben bitte in Zusatzzeile vornehmen)*

Angaben zu Sonstige

Hinweis: Die Eröffnungsbilanz ist gemäß § 5b Abs. 1 Satz 5 EStG nach amtlich vorgeschriebenen Datensatz durch Datenfernübertragung zu übermitteln.

7. Angaben zur Anmeldung und Abführung der Umsatzsteuer

7.1 Summe der Umsätze (geschätzt)	im Jahr der Betriebseröffnung EUR	im Folgejahr EUR
	6000	8000

7.3 Kleinunternehmer-Regelung

[X] Der auf das Kalenderjahr hochgerechnete Gesamtumsatz wird die Grenze des § 19 Abs. 1 UStG voraussichtlich nicht überschreiten. Es wird die Kleinunternehmer-Regelung in Anspruch genommen.
In Rechnungen wird keine Umsatzsteuer gesondert ausgewiesen und es kann kein Vorsteuerabzug geltend gemacht werden.
Hinweis: Angaben zu Tz. 7.8 sind nicht erforderlich; Umsatzsteuer-Voranmeldungen sind grundsätzlich nicht zu übermitteln.

[ ] Der auf das Kalenderjahr hochgerechnete Gesamtumsatz wird die Grenze des § 19 Abs. 1 UStG voraussichtlich nicht überschreiten. Es wird auf die Anwendung der Kleinunternehmer-Regelung verzichtet.
Die Besteuerung erfolgt nach den allgemeinen Vorschriften des Umsatzsteuergesetzes **für mindestens fünf Kalenderjahre** (§ 19 Abs. 2 UStG); Umsatzsteuer-Voranmeldungen sind monatlich in elektronischer Form authentifiziert zu übermitteln.

7.8 Soll-/Istversteuerung der Entgelte

Ich berechne die Umsatzsteuer nach [ ] vereinbarten Entgelten (**Sollversteuerung**).

oder

[ ] vereinnahmten Entgelten. Ich beantrage hiermit die **Istversteuerung**, weil

[ ] der auf das Kalenderjahr hochgerechnete Gesamtumsatz für das Gründungsjahr voraussichtlich nicht mehr als 500.000 EUR betragen wird.

[ ] ich von der Verpflichtung, Bücher zu führen und auf Grund jährlicher Bestandsaufnahmen regelmäßig Abschlüsse zu machen, nach § 148 Abgabenordnung (AO) befreit bin.

[ ] ich Umsätze ausführe, für die ich als Angehöriger eines freien Berufs im Sinne von § 18 Abs. 1 Nr. 1 des Einkommensteuergesetzes weder buchführungspflichtig bin noch freiwillig Bücher führe.

ANSWER KEY

UNIT 4

Exercise 1

a
1 A mobile phone sales shop.
2 VAT, trade tax, corporation tax
3 partnerships, corporations/limited companies
4 6%: the difference between being taxed as a partnership and a corporation
8-9%: church tax
15%: corporation tax
€ 24,500: tax-free allowance for partnerships

b
1 forms (alternative: types)
2 entity
3 levied
4 assessed
5 significant
6 liability
7 trading

Exercise 2

a

	sole proprietorship	civil law partnership	ordinary partnership	limited partnership
minimum capital	no	no	no	no
liability	full	full	full	limited
red tape	little	little	substantial	substantial

	limited partnership with limited company as general partner	small private limited company	private limited company	public limited company
minimum capital	yes	yes	yes	yes
liability	limited	limited	limited	limited
red tape	substantial	little*	little*	substantial

*using a model document

Exercise 3
1 Every business must pay trade tax, except self-employed professionals, farming, forestry and non-profit organisations.
2 Trade tax is a local tax collected by municipalities.
3 3.5%

Exercise 4
1 g 2 d 3 e 4 i 5 h 6 b 7 a 8 c 9 j 10 f

Exercise 5

		company's profit
	+	add-backs
	−	deductions
(if applicable)	−	tax-free amounts
	=	trade earnings
	x 3.5%	basic trade tax rate
	=	trade tax assessment base
	x	trade tax factor
	=	**trade tax**

Exercise 6
1 13 March 2028
Best regards
2 1 March 2032
Kind regards
3 January 3, 2025 (AE) or 1 March 2025 (BE)
Dear Madam or Sir
4 Dear Professor Durand
With kind regards

Exercise 7

		€ 100,000 (profit)
	−	€ 24,500 (tax-free amount)
	=	€ 75,500 (trade earnings)
	x 3.5%	(basic trade tax rate)
	=	€ 2,642 (trade tax assessment base)
	x	410% (trade tax factor)
	=	**€ 10,832.20**

Exercise 9
1 G   2 I+G   3 G   4 I   5 I   6 I   7 I

Exercise 10
1 assets   2 liabilities   3 owners'   4 retained
5 current   6 non-current   7 intangible
8 current   9 non-current   10 expenses
11 activities   12 reporting

Exercise 11
1 g   2 l   3 i   4 d   5 n   6 m   7 j   8 a   9 k
10 b   11 e   12 h   13 f   14 c

Exercise 12

upward movement	downward movement	other
to increase	to decrease	to fluctuate
to reach a peak	to hit a low	to remain steady
to take off	to slump	

Exercise 15
1 provision   2 deduction   3 add-back   4 liability
5 assess   6 levy   7 trade   8 corporation
9 entity   10 asset

UNIT 5

Exercise 1
a

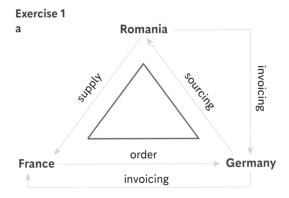

b 1 intra-Community supply   2 intra-Community acquisition   3 zero-rate   4 frontiers   5 triangulation

c
1 VAT accounting in dealings with the EU.
2 It is not involved in the supply.
3 The Romanian company will make a VAT-inclusive supply.
4 As long as the three companies involved are all in the EU.

d 1 F   2 F   3 F   4 T   5 F

e
Red tape (from the red tape used to bind official government documents in the 18th century) refers to time-consuming bureaucracy, involving excessive formality, routine and procedure. In the context of Huan's remark, red tape can be minimised by having business with the EU handled by their German subsidiary, thus avoiding the hassle of registering for VAT in every country, and taking advantage of intra-Community transactions, including triangulation, as needed.

Exercise 2
a
A distance sale is a transaction that does not involve face-to-face contact, such as online, telephone or mail orders.
Electronic services are IT technology-based, automated services provided by using the internet, cables or satellites. Examples include downloading apps, website hosting, distance learning, online gaming and streaming.
b
The reverse charge mechanism is a B2B concept that shifts the responsibility for paying VAT from the supplier to the buyer. It is meant to reduce the administrative and compliance burden on foreign suppliers providing services in countries where they are not present. Without it, they would typically be required to register in the customer's country for VAT purposes, collect and pay it locally. This can be time-consuming and difficult. There is no loss for customers as they can deduct the VAT they account for (input VAT). Reverse charge follows the idea that goods and services should be taxed where they are consumed.
c
1 € 109. The maximum limit to be able to deliver goods without paying local VAT is € 10,000. Any company that sells more than € 10,000 in goods to other EU countries during the previous financial year must apply the VAT rate of the country of destination. Assuming a "large online retailer" exceeds this limit, they have to charge Dutch VAT.
2 The Finnish supplier must charge Swedish (not Finnish) VAT.
3 As Joao's company is registered in Portugal, he has to charge his Danish customer Portuguese VAT.
4 As the German craftsman does not exceed the limit, he can charge German VAT.
5 German VAT applies (B2C) if Gina does not make more than € 10,000 a year abroad. Otherwise, Hungarian VAT applies, for which she can account for using the one stop shop (OSS).

ANSWER KEY

Exercise 5
a
1 Residency and tax liability
2 To prevent profit shifting and tax avoidance in related entity transactions
3 Exploiting gaps and mismatches in tax rules to shift profits artificially

b
1 residence, source
2 183
3 permanent establishment
4 credit, exemption
5 tax avoidance, tax evasion
6 transfer pricing
7 tax haven
8 base erosion, profit shifting

c
A permanent establishment is a fixed place of business with a sufficient presence to be subject to taxation.

Exercise 9
1 base erosion and profit shifting (BEPS)
2 business to business (B2B)
3 business to consumer (B2C)
4 double taxation agreement (DBA)
5 European Union (EU)
6 International Monetary Fund (IMF)
7 one stop shop (OSS)
8 Organisation for Economic Co-operation and Development (OECD)
9 telecommunications, broadcasting & electronic (TBE)
10 value-added tax (VAT)

UNIT 6

Exercise 1
1
- are independent.
- only work for one company.

2 fairly present a company's financial standing.
3 a crime might have occurred.
4 are mistakes of a significant nature. | potentially draw a false picture of a company's standing.
5 stakeholders.

Exercise 2
1 authorization and approval processes
2 information technology   3 financial reporting
4 fraud

1 financial transactions
2 cybersecurity
3 whistleblower program

Exercise 3
1 f   2 h   3 i   4 g   5 a   6 c   7 j   8 b   9 d   10 e

Exercise 4
1 UK: UKGAAP, IFRS (if applicable), International Standards on Auditing (ISAs UK)
US: US GAAP, Public Company Accounting Oversight Board (PCAOB)
Germany: HGB, IFRS (if applicable), EU-Abschlussprüferverordnung, Deutsche Grundsätze ordnungsmäßiger Abschlussprüfung des Instituts der Wirtschaftsprüfer (IDW)

Exercise 6
a 1 c   2 e   3 a   4 b   5 d

Exercise 7
1 pie chart   2 table   3 bar chart   4 line graph

Exercise 10
E: greenhouse gas emissions, waste management
S: headcount, employee turnover, gender diversity, lost time incidents
G: board composition, audit committee

Exercise 12
data, form, bonus, group, parent company, minutes, commission, rate, instalment, tax return, subsidiary, to take over

USEFUL PHRASES

The phrases below will be useful tools in your work. Highlight phrases which are particularly relevant to you and look at them regularly to help you remember them.

Additionally, you will find interactive exercises in the **Cornelsen Lernen App** expanding on the Useful Phrases provided in this book.

MEETING FOR THE FIRST TIME

Meeting & greeting
- Good morning, Mr Smith. How are you?
- I'm Klaus Müller. Nice to meet you.
- My name is Agata Beres. Pleased to meet you.
- This is my assistant, Sumiko Ito.
- May I introduce you to my partner in this firm, Mr Wang?

Offering hospitality
- Would you like something to drink?
- Can I offer you a cup of coffee?
- May I offer you a glass of water?
- Please help yourself to milk and sugar.

Small talk
- How was your journey/flight?
- How do you like your hotel?
- Did you find us alright? / Did you have any trouble finding us?
- Is this your first time in Germany? / Is this your first visit to Berlin?
- Terrible weather today, isn't it?

GIVING SHORT ANSWERS

- Sorry, do you speak English? – Certainly. What can I do for you?
- Can I just read that back to you: … – That's correct.
- Would Wednesday at 9 o'clock suit you? – Unfortunately, it doesn't. How about …?
- May I have your phone number? – Of course, it's …
- Is that acceptable to you? – I think so.
- Have you already been assigned a tax number? – Yes, I have.
- Did you have a tax advisor in the past? – No, I didn't.
- Will you ask your employer? – Yes, I will.

GIVING ADVICE

- You must file your tax return by 31 May.
- You have to enclose receipts.
- You ought to do it electronically.
- You should consider paying later.
- I (would) suggest calling your tax officer.
- I (would) suggest that I write to your tax office.
- I (would) recommend filing an appeal.
- I (would) recommend that you do not react.

USEFUL PHRASES

BEING MORE OR LESS FORMAL

Formal
- I would advise you to accept the decision.
- I recommend that you pay the penalty.
- Perhaps you could talk to your employer.
- I suggest that you get a confirmation from your payroll department.
- I think you'd better clarify your status.

Informal
- I'd accept it.
- I think you should pay the penalty.
- Why don't you talk to your boss?
- If I were you, I'd get a confirmation from the people in payroll.
- You should clarify this!

SINGPOSTING

- First of all, let us think about …
- Then, we need to …
- Next, you have to decide …
- Finally, we have to complete …
- Let's start with item three.
- Let's look at page four.
- Let's move on to section five.

EMAIL WRITING

Salutations
- Dear Sir or Madam
- Dear Madam/Sir
- To whom it may concern
- Dear Ms Hudson
- Dear Mr Hernandez
- Dear Jennifer
- Dear project team
- Dear all
- Hi Tim
- Annie

Closings
- Yours faithfully (BE)
- Yours sincerely/truly/cordially (BE)
- Sincerely/Truly/Cordially (yours) (AE)
- Kind/Best regards
- Best wishes

HOLDING MEETINGS, TELE- AND VIDEOCONFERENCES

Opening, chairing and closing
- Good morning, everybody.
- Can we start?
- Let's get down to business.
- Who's going to take the minutes?
- The purpose of our conference is …
- Our aim today is …
- There are three items on the agenda.
- Ali, would you like to start?
- Anything to add, Agniezska?
- Let's move on to the next item.
- Let me summarize the main points.
- Is there any other business?
- OK, thank you for all your contributions.

Taking part
- In my opinion …
- To my mind …
- In my view …
- I think / believe / suppose / assume / guess …
- I agree with you.
- I'm with Fatma on this.
- I'm afraid I can't agree with that.
- I see it rather differently.
- Can I just say at this point that …
- May I just come back to a point that Jim made?
- I didn't quite catch that.
- Do you see what I mean?
- Let me put it another way.

DESCRIBING TRENDS AND DEVELOPMENTS

Speaking about increase
- There has been a sharp increase in prices.
- We have seen a significant rise in turnover.
- Sales shot up after last year's update.
- Order numbers skyrocketed when a new version was announced.
- They reached a peak in March.

Speaking about stagnation
- Prices were stable in the last quarter.
- The tax burden remained steady at 25%.
- Corporate taxation stayed the same in the last ten years.
- Tax rates fluctuated considerably.

Speaking about decrease
- Profits decreased slightly.
- Figures gradually fell over the last years and bottomed out in 2025.
- The share price slumped when the CEO resigned.
- Bonus payments plunged due to poor performance.
- They hit a low in 2025.

CORRESPONDENCE

STANDARD PHRASES

When drafting correspondence, remember to
- keep it short and simple.
- capitalize the first word after the salutation.
- do not use contractions in formal settings.

Replying and referencing
- Thank you for your letter/email of 10 June 2028.
- With reference to your letter/email of 10 June 2029.
- Further to our phone call/meeting/talk of today/yesterday/10 October 2025, … .
- I would like to reply to your enquiry as follows: …
- Letters: Please find enclosed the documents (for your information/files / for review/approval/execution).
- Emails: Please find attached the documents (for your information/files / for review/approval/execution).
- I/We enclose/attach the documents.

Providing information
- We would like to inform you that we filed your tax return yesterday.
- We are pleased to inform you that you will receive a refund of € … .
- You may appeal the tax notice by 30 November 2027.
- We regret to inform you that the tax office declined the appeal.
- We are sorry to inform you that the tax office imposed a late payment/filing penalty/fine.

Requesting action
- Please act by 31 October. / submit the documents by 31 October.
- Please fill in/out (AE) the form.
- Please review the entries.
- Please return the questionnaire/sign and the enclosed statement.
- We would be grateful/appreciate it if you could give us information about …

Closing remarks
- Please do not hesitate to contact us if you have any further questions.
- We look forward to hearing from you. / meeting/working with you.
- Thank you for your assistance.

SAMPLE EMAILS

Dear Ms Ramdeen

Thank you for your enquiry.

We are a medium-sized accounting firm with six tax advisors, two public accountants, and a team of 30 staff. We advise on both personal and corporate taxation.

We would be happy to assist you.

Yours sincerely

…

ENGLISH FOR TAX PROFESSIONALS

Dear Ms Ling

We attach our letter of engagement. Please sign and return it if you agree to its terms.

We look forward to working with you.

Yours sincerely

…

Dear Mr Petrovic

With reference to your enquiry of 15 June 2028, we are pleased to provide information about corporate structures in Germany.

There are various types of partnerships and limited companies you can choose from. This depends on what you expect and are prepared to afford in terms of costs and risks. Capital, liability, red tape and taxes are some aspects to take into account.

Please find attached an overview.

We look forward to advising you.

Yours sincerely

…

Dear Mr Dudziak

Thank you for your email.

Your trade tax will amount to € 10,832.20.

Regarding relocation, there are several municipalities near Berlin with a lower trade tax factor. These include Schönefeld (240%), Zossen (270%), Ahrensfelde (300%), and Beelitz (306%).

If you have any further questions, please do not hesitate to contact me.

Yours sincerely

…

GLOSSARY

ACCRUALS/PROVISIONS/RESERVES

Accruals are revenues and expenses recognized by a company but not yet recorded in their accounts. They occur before an exchange of money resolves a transaction. **Provisions** are created to cover a present or future liability. **Reserves** are part of a company's profits, which have been kept aside to strengthen its financial position in the future and cover any losses. They are a part of retained earnings and thus belong to a company's equity. Reserves are made after paying taxes but before paying dividends (whereas retained earnings are what is left after paying dividends to stockholders). IAS 37 defines **four types of debt or liability**.

Liabilities (1) are certain, including their amount and timing. They appear on the balance sheet. Example: bills received.
Contingent liabilities (2) are uncertain to occur (probability <50%). They are not recorded on the balance sheet, but in the notes. Example: having issued a guarantee for a customer.
Provisions (3) are liabilities that will probably occur (probability >50%). They are recorded on the balance sheet. Example: a creditor has announced to make claims under an issued guarantee.
Accruals (4) are liabilities that will occur, but their amounts might change slightly. They appear on the balance sheet under "other payables". Example: costs of statutory audits, holiday pay for employees.

AMORTIZATION/DEPRECIATION

Process of reducing the book value of an **intangible/fixed asset** over a specific number of years.

CASH FLOW STATEMENT

Summarizes the amount of cash (+ cash equivalents, i.e. short-term investments that can readily be converted into cash) entering and leaving a company. It is broken down into **operating**, **investing** and **financing activities**. The **operating activities** include cash from business activities, i.e. how much is generated from a company's products or services. **Investing activities** include cash from a company's investments, such as assets and loans. Cash from **financing activities** includes cash from investors and banks, as well as the way cash is paid to shareholders, including dividends, payments for stock repurchases, and repayment of loans.

DISTANCE SALES

Sales without face-to-face contact. Examples include online, mail or telephone orders.

LEDGER

A book in which a business writes down the amounts of money it spends and receives. The **general ledger** is the accounting transaction record of all the balance sheet and income statement balances of a business. The five main types of general ledger accounts are asset account, liability account, expense account, revenue account, and equity account.

RETURN ON CAPITAL EMPLOYED (ROCE)

A financial ratio that is used to measure the profitability of a company and the efficiency with which it uses its capital. It measures how good a business is at generating profits from capital.

RETURN ON NET ASSETS (RONA)

A measure of financial performance calculated as net profit divided by the sum of fixed assets and net working capital. It shows how well a company and its management are deploying assets in economically valuable ways. A high ratio result indicates more earnings out of money invested in assets. RONA is also used to assess how well a company is performing compared to others in its industry.

STATEMENT OF ACTIVITIES

A financial statement prepared by charities/non-profit organizations, disclosing their income and expenses. It is similar to an income statement and depicts funding sources, programme and administrative costs, as well as restrictions imposed on assets by donors.

STATEMENT OF CHANGES IN EQUITY

A statement that shows the amounts of equity the owners have at the beginning and at the end of the reporting period.

STATEMENT OF COMPREHENSIVE INCOME

Comprehensive income includes **net income** (profit or loss) + **other comprehensive income** (OCI). This is income not yet realized, i.e. revenues, expenses, gains, and losses on, for example, securities, currency and pension liability adjustments.

STATEMENT OF EXPENSES

A presentation of expenses by their functions (e.g. programme, development and fund raising expenses), usually included in the statement of activities of a charity/non-profit organization.

YIELD

The income an investment returns over time, typically expressed as a percentage. **Return**, on the other hand, is the amount that was gained or lost on an investment over time, usually expressed as a money figure.

A-Z WORDLIST

A
accountability   Rechenschaft, Verantwortung
to **adhere to** sth   etw. befolgen, einhalten
AGM (annual general meeting)   Jahreshauptversammlung
to **align** sth   etw. in Einklang bringen
allowance   *hier:* Freibetrag
to **assess** sth   etw. festsetzen
assessment   Beurteilung
assets   Aktiva, Vermögenswerte
to **assign** sth   etw. zuweisen
attestation   Testat

B
band   *hier:* Tarifstufe
base erosion and profit shifting   Gewinnverkürzung und Gewinnverlagerung
to **be on high alert**   in hoher Alarmbereitschaft sein
bogus self-employment   Scheinselbständigkeit
to **breach** sth   etw. verletzen

C
capital gains tax, flat-rate withholding tax   Abgeltungssteuer
care insurance   Pflegeversicherung
cash accounting   Einnahmenüberschussrechnung
column   Spalte
commitment   Verpflichtung
conduct   (*hier:* berufsrechtlich relevantes) Handeln, Verhalten
confidentiality   Geheimhaltung, Vertraulichkeit
contribution   Beitrag
COO (Chief Operating Officer)   Vorstand für das operative Geschäft
to **cook the books**   Bücher frisieren
corporation tax   Körperschaftsteuer
credit   *hier:* Anrechnung
current assets   Umlaufvermögen
current liabilities   kurzfristige Verbindlichkeiten
country-of-destination principle   Bestimmungslandprinzip
country-of-origin principle   Ursprungslandprinzip

D
damages (pl.)   Schadensersatz
deductions   Abzüge
to **deem** sth   etw. ansehen/betrachten
to **defer** sth   etw. verlagern
demand   Nachfrage
to **derive** sth   *hier:* etw. erzielen
directive   Richtlinie
to **discharge**   *hier:* entlasten
discreditable   unrühmlich
distance sales   Fernverkäufe
to **divert** sth   etw. umleiten
divestiture   Entflechtung
domestic   inländisch

E
eligible   berechtigt
employee allowance, employee standard deduction   Arbeitnehmerpauschbetrag
to **enhance** sth   etw. verbessern
entity   Körperschaft, juristische Person
estate planning   Nachfolgeplanung
to **estimate** sth   etw. schätzen
to **exceed** sth   etw. überschreiten
exemption   *hier:* Freistellung
expiry   Ablauf
to **exploit** so/sth   jmdn./etw. ausnutzen

F
fee schedule   Gebührentabelle
to **file an appeal**, to **appeal**   Einspruch einlegen
fine   Bußgeld
forensic accounting   forensische Wirtschaftsprüfung
fraud   Betrug

G
to **go into hiding**   untertauchen
group company   Konzerngesellschaft

I
incentive   Anreiz
income-related expenses   Werbungskosten
to **incur** sth   etw. verursachen
indemnity insurance   Berufshaftpflichtversicherung
to **inflate** sth   etw. aufblähen
initial consultation   Erstberatung
instructions   Weisungen
intellectual property   geistiges Eigentum
(intra-Community) acquisition   (innergemeinschaftlicher) Erwerb
(intra-Community) supply   (innergemeinschaftliche) Lieferung

J
jointly   gemeinsam

L
layer   *hier:* Ebene
to **levy** sth   etw. erheben
liability   Haftung
liabilities (pl.)   Passiva, Verbindlichkeiten
loan   Kredit, Darlehn
loophole   Schlupfloch

M
to **mandate** sth   etw. vorschreiben
to **mask** sth   etw. verschleiern
material   *hier:* wesentlich
to **misrepresent** sth   etw. falsch darstellen
misstatement   Falschdarstellung
municipal authority   Gemeindeverwaltung

N
non-current assets   Anlagevermögen
non-current liabilities   langfristige Verbindlichkeiten

O
occupational disability insurance   Berufsunfähigkeitsversicherung
opinion   *hier:* Gutachten
to **opt for** sth   sich für etw. entscheiden

P

permanent establishment Betriebsstätte
personal allowance Grundfreibetrag
personal liability insurance Privathaftpflichtversicherung
to **plunge** abstürzen
policy Richtlinie
to **pose a challenge** eine Herausforderung darstellen
professional indemnity insurance Berufshaftpflichtversicherung

R

to **reach a peak** einen Höchststand erreichen
reasonableness Angemessenheit
to **recognise sth** hier: etw. realisieren
red tape Verwaltungsaufwand, Bürokratie
regulation Verordnung
remuneration Vergütung
to **reprimand so** jmdn. verwarnen
residence Wohnsitz
retained earnings (pl.) Gewinnvortrag
to **retain sth** etw. ein-/zurückbehalten
reverse charge Umkehrung der Steuerschuldnerschaft
royalty Lizenzgebühr

S

sampling Stichproben
to **schedule so/sth** jmdn./etw. einplanen, (terminlich) eintragen
scrutiny Prüfung, Untersuchung
sick pay Lohnfortzahlung
to **skyrocket** hochschnellen
to **slump** einbrechen
small entrepreneur Kleinunternehmer
source Quelle
to **source sth** etw. beziehen
special expenses Sonderausgaben
statutory gesetzlich
stakeholder Akteur*in, Interessenvertreter*in
to **submit sth** etw. übermitteln, einreichen
subsidiary Tochtergesellschaft
to **suit so** jmdm. passen
supervisory board Aufsichtsrat
supervisory body/watchdog Aufsichtsbehörde
surcharge Zuschlag, Zusatzbeitrag
sustainability Nachhaltigkeit
sustainability reporting Nachhaltigkeitsberichterstattung

T

tax (assessment) notice Steuerbescheid
tax avoidance Steuervermeidung
tax bracket, filing status (AE) Steuerklasse
threshold Grenze
tax evasion Steuerhinterziehung
thorough gründlich
tier Stufe
to **tighten** hier: verschärfen
trade tax Gewerbesteuer
transfer pricing Verrechnungspreise
transitory item durchlaufender Posten
triangulation Dreiecksgeschäft
true and fair view ein den tatsächlichen Verhältnissen entsprechendes Bild
trustee Treuhänder
turnover Umsatz

U

uniform rate einheitlicher Satz

V

vulnerability hier: Schwäche

W

to **walk sb through sth** mit jmdm. etw. durchgehen

Z

to **zero-rate sth** etw. umsatzsteuerfrei behandeln

TROUBLESHOOTING

much & many	uncountable & countable	**much** money, **many** problems
who & which	people & objects	The client **who** … | The file **which** …
if & when	condition & time	**If** I see you later, I'll give you the documents. = *(I don't know whether I'll see you.)* **When** I see you later, I'll give you the documents. = *(I know I'll see you.)*
by & until	deadline & period	I need this **by** tomorrow. | I'll work **until** 8.
since & for	point of time & period of time	I've been running my business **since** 2025. / **for** three years.
lend & borrow	give & get	The bank **lends** me money. I **borrow** money from the bank.
meet	We'll meet ~~us~~ on Monday.	We'll **meet** on Monday.
discuss	Let's discuss ~~about~~ your bookkeeping.	Let's **discuss** your bookkeeping.
overtake	You could ~~overtake~~ the company.	You could **take over** the company.
theme	This is an important ~~theme~~.	This is an important **topic/subject**.
million	It costs 1 ~~mio~~.	It costs 1 **m**.
prove	I'll ~~prove~~ the account.	I'll **check** the account.
control	I'll ~~control~~ the account.	I'll **check** the account.
critic	There's been a lot of ~~critic~~.	There's been a lot of **criticism**.
jurisdiction	According to the ~~jurisdiction~~ of the Finance Court …	According to the **decision** of the Finance Court …
paragraph	According to ~~paragraph~~ 104 …	According to **section** 104 …
mandate	I'm handling a new ~~mandate~~.	I'm handling a new **case/matter**.
mandate	I'm ~~mandated~~ by ABC company.	I'm **instructed** by ABC company.
damage	This caused ~~many damages~~.	This caused **much/a lot of damage**.
training	We offer ~~many trainings~~.	We offer **much/a lot of training**. / **many training sessions/courses/programs**.
he/she (when referring to offices/ authorities/courts)	~~He~~ said … / ~~She~~ decided …	**It/They** said/decided …

GERUND

Example: *I look forward to hear**ing** from you.*

Pay attention to words and expressions that are followed by a gerund (you need to add **-ing** to the verb, but do not confuse this with the present progressive tense).
Verbs often used in consulting are **suggest** and **recommend**. Here are a few others: **admit, avoid, consider, deny, dislike, discuss, enjoy, finish, give up, imagine, involve, justify, mention, mind, practise, risk**.
Further expressions include: **be busy, be/get used to, don't mind, how/what about, object to, there's no point, worth**.
Prepositions, both on their own (**after, against, before, by, instead of, like, than + without**) and in connection with certain verbs, nouns or adjectives (all prepositions) are also followed by a gerund.

Examples:
- You should **avoid paying** too much. *(verb)*
- **Before making** a decision, we should carefully assess the situation. *(preposition)*
- Success will **depend on finding** a loophole. *(verb + preposition)*
- There is a **risk of losing** your investment. *(noun + preposition)*
- You are **responsible for informing** your tax office immediately. *(adjective + preposition)*

SPELLING

a**ccomm**odate	ac**qu**ire	a**ddre**ss	a**sses**sment	coll**eague**
column**n**	co**mmittee**	co**mmitt**ed	depend**a**nt	ex**cee**d
grateful	**gu**arantee	i**mm**ediate	independ**e**nt	ju**dgm**ent
l**o**se *(verb)*	l**oo**se *(adjective)*	main**te**nance	o**cc**asion	o**cc**u**rr**ence
perso**nn**el	po**sse**ssion	privi**le**ge	su**cc**e**ss**ful	thre**sh**old

STRESS AND INTONATION

con**vict**	**con**vict	de**sert**	**des**ert	sus**pect**	**sus**pect
*(verb	noun)*	*(verb	noun)*	*(verb	noun)*
perfect	per**fect**	in**valid**	**in**valid	com**plex**	**com**plex
*(adjective	verb)*	*(adjective	noun)*	*(adjective	noun)*

COMMAS

Commas can be used beyond established rules to **change** or **clarify meaning**:

Let's eat, mum! → *Let's eat mum!*

- The accountant said the client is great to work with.
- The accountant, said the client, is great to work with.
- The accountant talked to Tim and Alex then called the tax office.
- The accountant talked to Tim and Alex, then called the tax office.
- The accountant talked to Tim, and Alex then called the tax office.
- Mary Ann Lee and Kim will attend the meeting.
- Mary Ann, Lee, and Kim will attend the meeting.
- Mary, Ann, Lee, and Kim will attend the meeting.

ACRONYMS AND KEY VERBS

AICPA	American Institute of Certified Public Accountants		**IMF**	International Monetary Fund
AP	accounts payable		**IRS**	Internal Revenue Service
AR	accounts receivable		**LLC/P**	limited liability company/partnership
B2B	business to business		**LTD**	private limited company
B2C	business to consumer		**MTT**	municipal trade tax
BEPS	base erosion and profit shifting		**NI**	net income
CAP	capital		**OCI**	other comprehensive income
CFC	controlled foreign company		**OECD**	Organisation for Economic Co-operation and Development
CG	corporate governance		**OSS**	one stop shop
CGT	capital gains tax		**P&L**	profit and loss
CIT	corporate income tax		**PAYE**	pay-as-you-earn
COGS	cost of goods sold		**PE**	permanent establishment
CPA	Certified Public Accountant		**PIT**	personal income tax
CRS	Common Reporting Standard		**PLC**	public limited company
CSR	Corporate Social Responsibility		**REIT**	real estate investment trust
DTA/T	double taxation agreement/treaty		**RETT**	real estate transfer tax
EBIT(DA)	earnings before interest, tax (depreciation and amortization)		**ROI**	return on investment
			ROCE	return on capital employed
ESG	environmental, social & governance		**ROE**	return on equity
FASB	Financial Accounting Standards Board		**RONA**	return on net assets
GAAP	generally accepted accounting principles		**SEC**	Securities & Exchange Commission
GDP	gross domestic product		**SOX**	Sarbanes-Oxley
GL	general ledger		**SPE/V**	special-purpose entity/vehicle
GST	goods and services tax		**SPR**	small profits rate
IAS	International Accounting Standards		**TBE**	telecommunications, broadcasting & electronic
ICAEW	Institute of Chartered Accountants of England & Wales		**VAT**	value-added tax
IFRS	International Financial Reporting Standard		**WHT**	withholding tax

to **assess**	We will **assess** your case and get back to you asap.	beurteilen
to **assign**	You could **assign** these claims to your creditors.	abtreten
to **bill/invoice**	We will **bill/invoice** you monthly.	eine Rechnung stellen
to **calculate**	We **calculated** your refund.	ausrechnen, berechnen
to **capitalise**	You can **capitalise** these expenses.	aktivieren
to **defer**	We would advise **deferring** payment.	verlagern, verschieben
to **fine**	The tax office can **fine** you for late filings or payments.	einen Zuschlag erheben
to **incur**	You will **incur** additional fees.	anfallen, auslösen, verursachen
to **monitor**	Please **monitor** these accounts.	überwachen, beobachten
to **offset**	You can **offset** these claims.	verrechnen
to **reimburse**	You should **reimburse** your employees for travel expenses incurred.	erstatten
to **retain**	You can **retain** earnings.	einbehalten, vortragen